Praise for
Trust Me

Our world needs plenty of what *Trust Me* has to offer—the basic building blocks of integrity that every leader needs, regardless of the type of company or organization.

—ANDY ANDREWS, entertainer, author of *The Traveler's Gift*

In a world where the acronym CEO is quickly becoming synonymous with deceitful business practice, *Trust Me* offers an empowering alternative backed by timeless truth. This is a must-read for all veteran and aspiring business leaders.

—SCOTT JEFFREY, strategic advisor and author of *Journey to the Impossible*

Ron Potter understands that effective leaders need to fully appreciate the role emotional intelligence plays in the interpersonal relationships that are so important to employee morale and business success in the workplace.

—ARTIE BYRD, vice president of Kellogg's

Trust Me teaches leaders at all levels how to be effective by being compassionate but firm, flexible but tenacious, and humble but confident.

—WILLIAM SIGMUND II, M.D., vice president of Pfizer Pharmaceuticals

The concepts and tools [Ron Potter] has developed helps leaders shape their organization's culture and reflexes. We are a different and better company today as a result of this influence on our leaders and corporate culture.

—DAVID BRANDON, chairman and CEO of Domino's Pizza

Trust Me is a multivitamin for leaders. Hastings and Potter provide a lot for those who want to be healthy and capable. If you're looking for one mega-dosage on leadership, *trust me,* this is the book.

—BRUCE R. JOHNSON, directional strategist and author of the Next Level
    Leadership Series

Trust Me is the owner's manual for effective leaders.

—JOE QUESTEL, president and CEO of Questel & Associates

"Trust Me...explores new territory, provides actionable ideas, and demonstrates that leading with integrity is not only possible but absolutely necessary in the times in which we live."

—MARK SANBORN, president, National Speakers Association
and author of *The Fred Factor*

Whether people are in a leadership position or not, they should read this book.... If leaders applied just a few of these principles, the world would be a much better place.

—DR. RALPH MCCALL, company director and author

Nothing is more important than the investment in growing and keeping trust in our relationships and organizations. *Trust Me* offers a clear, insightful, inspirational application of the Beatitudes to current leadership practice.

—ANN MCGEE-COOPER, ED.D., business consultant, futurist,
and author of *You Don't Have to Go Home from Work Exhausted*

Ron Potter's approach to understanding leadership styles is as effective in developing a cohesive team as it is in helping an individual grow professionally.

—RUSS POTTS, plant manager, Bosch Braking Systems

I highly recommend *Trust Me*, as I know you can trust Wayne Hastings. I have known him as a friend, student, leader, and respected executive. In every area I have found him to be a man of his word and of God's Word.

—FLORENCE LITTAUER, speaker, author, and founder of the CLASSeminar

The greatest contributor to effective leadership is having a shared vision.... Ron Potter was instrumental in guiding my leadership team to understand and embrace such a shared vision.

—BOB SHEROFF, president of Global Biologics Supply Chain, Centocor, Inc.

The programs and the work we have done together [with Ron Potter] will carry me through my entire career. I think they call those "learnings for life."

—AL CAPLAN, MGI Pharma

Trust Me

Developing a Leadership Style **People Will Follow**

WAYNE HASTINGS
and RON POTTER

WATERBROOK
PRESS

TRUST ME
PUBLISHED BY WATERBROOK PRESS
2375 Telstar Drive, Suite 160
Colorado Springs, Colorado 80920
A division of Random House, Inc.

ISBN 1-57856-754-8

Library of Congress Cataloging-in-Publication Data
Hastings, Wayne.
   Trust me : developing a leadership style people will follow / Wayne A. Hastings and Ronald Potter.— 1st ed.
      p. cm.
   ISBN 1-57856-754-8
   1. Leadership—Religious aspects—Christianity. I. Potter, Ronald. II. Title.
BV4597.53.L43H37 2004
253—dc22   2003018955

Printed in the United States of America
2004—First Edition

10 9 8 7 6 5 4 3 2 1

Contents

Qualities of a trusted leader...

Humility

"Favored are those not full of themselves"—leaders who are open
and teachable...and invite the same qualities in others.

Development

"Favored are the realists"—leaders who accept the truth and know
how to train others to seize the benefits of adversity, loss, and change.

Commitment

"Favored are the steadfast"—leaders who know that reaching a greater
good requires a firm grip on the right values, causes, and goals.

Focus

"Favored are those desperate for excellence"—leaders
who do the right things at the right time in the right way.

Compassion

*"Favored are the caring"—leaders who serve the needs
of everyone in their organizations.*

Integrity

*"Favored are those with unshakable ethics"—leaders who hold
high moral values regardless of personal cost.*

Peacemaking

*"Favored are those who calm the waters"—leaders who remain steady
in storms and build teams that stick together.*

Endurance

*"Favored are those with fortitude"—leaders who overcome personal
doubts and setbacks to courageously stay the course.*

Acknowledgments

I would like to acknowledge the men who have been mentors in my life:

- My father, Charles Lee Potter (1920–1973), who built in the basic values of truth and honesty that have been the foundation of my life.
- Keith Hunt of InterVarsity Christian Fellowship, who guided my young life and early adult life in solid Christian training and development.
- C. E. (Bill) Bottum, president of Townsend and Bottum, Inc., who helped bring my Christian values into my business life.
- Joe Fisher, my partner at Orion International, who believed in me and showed me the ropes in my early days of consulting.
- Tom Webber (1948–2002), a fellow colleague who taught me much about the human mind and human behavior. I'll see you in heaven, Tom.

I would especially like to acknowledge my mother, who placed me in a position in which I could accept Jesus as my Lord and Savior, and my wife, Jill, who has journeyed with me through thirty-four years (and counting) of career development and entrepreneurial challenges.

—RON POTTER

I would like to acknowledge the people who have been leaders and mentors in my life:

- Pam, my wife and strongest advocate. Thank you for all you do to free me up to pursue my dreams (thirty-three years and counting).
- My children, Jennifer and Zachary. Thank you for your support, encouragement, and love.
- My father and mother, Ray and Catherine Hastings, who instilled in me the values of integrity, hard work, and endurance.

- Ron Potter, my friend and mentor, who first planted the seed of this book and without whom this book would still be in my head and dreams.
- Dan Benson, who first captured the vision and gave us hope and confidence.
- Scott Jeffrey, who coached me through the process.

—WAYNE HASTINGS

We would also like to acknowledge Bruce Barbour, for his early encouragement and instruction, and everyone at WaterBrook, especially Bruce Nygren, Jennifer Lonas, Don Pape, and Steve Cobb—what a team!

Foreword

A search for leadership and management books on Amazon.com reveals literally tens of thousands of titles. If you are like me, you have probably read many books on the subject, yet can cite only a few that have made a real difference in how we behave on a daily basis. I believe this book falls into that category.

Having been in the leadership development business for twenty-five years, including authoring two books on the subject, I can confidently say that few people ever become better leaders by reading a book, watching a video, or attending a seminar. We can learn *about* leadership doing those things, but rarely does deep personal change result. Occasionally a person may experience a significant emotional event that provides the impetus for change. But most of us need something more—much more. Provided you are willing to grow and change, this book provides that something extra that is missing in most leadership books. Allow me to explain.

Leadership is not something we grasp intellectually—like understanding algebra or learning to read a balance sheet—and one day exclaim, "Okay, I've got it!" Leadership development is more analogous to becoming a great carpenter, athlete, or musician. Knowledge gained in the field is important, but if that head knowledge is not applied consistently, little will change. Has anyone ever learned how to swim by reading a book?

Wayne Hastings and Ron Potter have put together a well thought out and superbly researched book on what real leadership is, based upon the thoughts and life of the greatest leader who ever lived. What I especially appreciate is that they have provided practical exercises they call "Change from the Inside Out" at the end of each chapter. Again, when it comes to leadership, knowledge without application is, for the most part, useless.

When we think about leadership, it is important to remember that it is not about being the boss or being a good manager. I have known many excellent managers who were train wrecks when it came to being effective leaders. Leadership is not what we do, it is who we are. Simply put, leadership is influence. Leadership involves influencing others for good, rousing others to action, and inspiring them to become the best they can be, as we work together toward common goals. By that definition, we are all leaders, because we all influence others. Everyone leaves a mark.

If leadership is about influence, doesn't it make sense—as Wayne and Ron chose to do—to look to the person who has influenced more people than anyone in history? Certainly, no intellectually honest person can deny Jesus Christ had and still has more influence than anyone who has ever lived. Fully one-third of the people on the planet call themselves "Christians." Christianity is far and away the largest faith system.

One of Jesus' greatest lectures is what we call the Sermon on the Mount. From those teachings, Wayne and Ron have drawn eight principles to guide us on our journey in leading others. These principles include humility, development, commitment, focus, compassion, integrity, peacemaking, and endurance. Each principle is a personal quality of character.

Leadership guru Warren Bennis has summed up his body of work by saying that "leadership is character in action." It is the right thing to do to be honest, humble, committed, and focused, and to follow each of the eight principles defined and discussed in this fine book. Leadership is doing the right thing. Character is doing the right thing. In the end, leadership development and character development are one.

Oftentimes, character and personality get confused and are used interchangeably. Personality is pretty well fixed by the age of six, and anyone can complete a simple inventory to determine his or her personality profile. Character, on the other hand, is our moral maturity, our developed moral muscles and commitment to doing the right thing even when we don't feel like it and there is a cost involved.

Character is dynamic and changes over time, either for better or worse. Unlike personality, character is not a set of traits fixed in time, hence the word *maturity*. As farmers are fond of saying, "You are either green and growing or ripe and rotting."

If you are truly committed to becoming a better leader, this book can provide you with the knowledge and a map to incorporate that knowledge into your personal character. If you are truly committed to change and continuous improvement, I encourage you to do the work Wayne and Ron suggest at the end of each chapter.

With persistence and steadfast commitment toward building your character and your leadership skills, in time you will discover that you no longer have to try to be a good leader; you will have become a good leader. You will not have to try to be a good person, you will have become a good person.

God's blessings to you on your journey.

—JIM HUNTER, author of the best-selling book *The Servant*

The Way of Trust

Steve seemed to have it all. He was tough, smart, disciplined, quick on his feet, and an effective strategist. He worked hard and could match anybody's résumé with an impressive list of business and personal skills. With all that Steve had going for him, why was he failing in his latest and greatest work assignment? Was there a way for him to pull out of his tailspin?

Before his success in business, Steve had been an Army Ranger. Listening to Steve was like listening to a Tom Clancy audio book, only this was the actual participant reminiscing in real time. Steve's Ranger training had prepared him to withstand almost anything, including extreme pain, in order to execute a mission. When Steve recalled his adventures, the look in his eyes assured his audience that if he had ever been captured even excessive torture might not have broken him. Steve might have chosen to die rather than disclose information to an enemy. This was one sharp, strong man—Rambo in a business suit.

Part of Steve's extensive Ranger training had included instruction in being a leader at any level of organizational structure. Steve understood both giving and taking orders. He knew how to take charge, size up the situation, and go after the objective.

Steve's boss, a vice president named Pat, had recruited Steve for a new assignment. Pat had a reputation for building successful organizations and had recently assumed responsibility for a whole new division in this sizable company. Pat strongly believed in building individuals and teams, and to accomplish this with his new team, Pat had hired me (Ron) as a leadership consultant to facilitate more personal discovery for himself and his fresh staff of elite leaders.

As part of my consulting approach, I had tested Pat's team to assess leadership performance. That's how I first met Steve. I'll never forget the afternoon I met with this man who was so discouraged that his whole demeanor drooped. His confidence eroding, Steve sat slumped in a chair. He was desperately looking for understanding and some help to regain his footing.

What had pierced the strength of this highly trained, combat-proven Ranger?

Steve's discouragement resulted from feedback he had just received from his peers on his leadership style and how it was affecting his ability to lead, to be trusted, and to be a good team member. He thought his leadership practices were sound, but his peers and "direct-reports" (those who reported to him directly) saw them as oppositional, competitive, and detrimental to the team's ability to function successfully.

Steve saw himself as a good, competent leader. He had been a member of one of the most elite, high-performance teams in the world—the Army Rangers. Now, as a successful businessman, he wanted more than anything to be a member of a high-performance team. Before I showed up, Steve assumed that he had made all the right moves, had all the right skills, and was doing just great, thank you! Now this devastating feedback from his team told him otherwise. He knew in his heart that he had the right stuff, so what was wrong?

What Steve didn't understand is that skill is only part of the equation. He did have many solid leadership attributes in place: He was committed and focused, had great integrity, and could endure difficulties. What Steve didn't understand was that some of his behavior and attitudes were offensive to coworkers. It didn't matter to them that he was an ex-Army Ranger and had great leadership qualities and a list of achievements to show for it. To them he seemed proud. Steve didn't understand the difference between being proud of your accomplishments and being perceived as kind of a cocky know-it-all. His air of superiority kept others from feeling they could trust him.

Once Steve began to exhibit a more humble attitude in response to his teammates' feedback and became more attentive to their accomplishments and strengths, trust began to build. Since Steve no longer felt the need to blow his own horn about his accomplishments, his coworkers—because they liked and trusted him more—began to express to him their pride in his accomplishments.

As is so often the case in today's business environment, Steve's team changed dramatically over time. The company went through a merger, Pat was enticed away by another company, and many of Steve's peers left in the merger downsizing. Steve's still there, however...as team leader.

Snoopy, Charlie Brown's irrepressible dog, once lamented, "It's not easy being head beagle." And in the wake of recent moral meltdowns at both high and low levels of corporate America, Snoopy's insight may be more on target now than ever before.

For those who still aspire to lead others well, however, the current leadership climate presents a great opportunity—especially for those who earnestly want to lead right. As never before—in all segments of society—we earnestly want to associate with people who are genuinely trustworthy.

"Whether in a corporation, a Scout troop, a public agency, or an entire nation, constituents seek four things: meaning or direction, trust in and from the leader, a sense of hope and optimism, and results."[1] Well said, Warren Bennis.

Trust is at the heart of any honest relationship. Building teams, leading organizations, and working with shareholders and customers require open, honest relationships.

A trusted style of leadership is what we offer in this book. Regardless of where you have been and what you have done—or even if you have no experience at all—you can become a leader worthy of trust. This leadership style will change you; it will change the lives of others around you; it will change companies and organizations.

Quality leadership is vitally important today, and many people work hard to improve their leadership skills. But all the training and technical skills, as important as they are, will not create an enduring, trusted leader.

How do you become a trusted leader? Is there a proven path that ensures you will be a leader others will follow?

ANOTHER STORY

Our friend Steve was not alone in realizing that his leadership style needed help.

Long before this book was even a dream, when I (Wayne) first met Ron, I realized he was a talented leader who would be a good man to know. At the time of our first meeting, I was a senior executive in the wholesale distribution industry. Over the years I had led teams and found some level of success, but I knew I had not discovered the secret of moving from being a good leader to a great leader.

Ron and I became friends, and I eventually accepted another executive position with a different firm. This new company was growing, and as we added additional executives to the team, we invited Ron to come help us with leadership training. Ron used the same approach with us as he did with Steve. My test results devastated me. Full of dismay and discouragement, I, like Steve, ended up in a face-to-face meeting with Ron.

I had thought I was an effective leader. Now, staring at my leadership-style scores, I was learning that I was a minor-leaguer at best. Difficult truths confronted me. If my leadership style did not change, my progress and the likelihood of future success were in jeopardy.

As a leader I was defined by my competitiveness, perfectionism, and avoidance of unpleasant reality. My team members saw me as combative and individualistic. I showed little need for affiliation with the team. I was not trusted. Clearly, I had much work to do on my leadership approach.

With kindness and obvious professionalism, Ron made me aware of my need for the incredible principles this book presents. I have made changes, and I believe I am a much stronger leader today than in the past. The principles have so influenced my life that I am now teaching them to leaders in a variety of organizations. I want as many people as possible to understand that a leadership style based on trust makes all the difference in achieving individual, team, and organizational success.

A Newfound Passion

The temptation I (Ron) face is to settle for claiming my title as "exalted consultant" and go smugly on to share all of my life-changing wisdom! But my coauthor and hundreds of clients and associates who know me would never let me get away with it. So now I need to share some of my own story, which reveals the real sources of any profound information and insights I've collected.

Several decades ago I had the good fortune of finding work as an engineer for a company led by an outstanding man named C. E. (Bill) Bottum. Bill was an out-of-the-box thinker—if you know what I mean—long before anybody even talked about thinking in or out of boxes.

About five years into my work for Bill, a change in how our firm was using subcontractors necessitated the hiring of a firm to help those of us in leadership roles improve our interpersonal relationship skills.

I had just finished designing a construction framework that required careful attention to where and how forces were applied. Coincidentally, at about the same time I was asked to fill out an assessment of my leadership style. Using the same testing instrument I would employ with both Steve and Wayne years later, I also received some sobering but eye-opening feedback from my peers, my direct-reports, and my boss.

That was half a lifetime ago, but I still remember thinking, *If I don't change some areas of my leadership style, I'm never going to experience the success in life that I desire.*

Equally illuminating to me was the realization that an instrument designed to examine my leadership style could be just as scientifically valid as the engineering design work I had recently completed. A whole string of lights turned on for me. With the help of an assessment tool, I could examine and analyze the overall forces that were driving my leadership style, and I could clearly see how that style was affecting those around me. Additionally, I could dig into the details to better understand which elements of my style were applying stress and what happened as a result of that stress. I could then reinforce those areas of my style that needed buttressing, just as I had designed additional reinforcements to assure a successful engineering project.

These insights eventually resulted in a dramatic career change for me. I realized that insight into what makes leaders "tick" could have dramatic, positive ramifications not only for the leaders themselves but also for the many people they influence. Entire organizations could become more self-aware and focused in the pursuit of their vision, mission, and goals. And the individuals involved could experience a whole lot more enjoyment and career satisfaction along the way.

But my greatest light-bulb moment was yet to come—also courtesy of Bill Bottum.

Several years later I, like many, many others, became enamored with a hot new business book titled *In Search of Excellence*. I remember going to see Bill, eager to tell him about the book and share with him what I had learned from it. I found that Bill was a few pages ahead of me. Not only was he already familiar with the book, but as we discussed the conclusions of the authors Thomas Peters and Robert Waterman Jr., Bill informed me that in his opinion the authors had just recovered some ancient, time-tested truths about leadership.

Bill reached into a desk drawer and showed me a chart he had created, the result of a lifetime of developing what he called "the guiding principles." Bill then showed me how the main points of *In Search of Excellence* clearly aligned with his principles. This book is based on the same basic guiding principles. And these principles have an unexpected origin.

A Surprising Source

Two thousand years ago a sizable group of people were desperately looking for a new leader. They were caught in an unfortunate trap, living under a cruel local and national dictatorship. They were looking for someone who would lead them away from tyranny toward peace, harmony, and better personal circumstances. Lower taxes would be nice too!

Then a remarkable young man came on the scene. Many thought he was the one who could lead such an overthrow. This young leader assembled a team. As is often the case, the team members started fighting among themselves, scheming for the top positions in the coming "new order." Like many aspiring leaders, they assumed that being in charge meant climbing the ladder, fighting for an exalted position on the company organizational chart, assuming power, taking control, gaining privilege, enjoying prestige, and having others serve them.

One day the young leader asked for some time with his team members. Would this be the day he announced his plan to lead the rebellion against the oppressors? Would he hand out the choice assignments in the new regime?

He took his men aside and said in so many words, "Listen, guys, true leadership is different from anything you've seen or heard. It's not about skill, power, or control. It's all about developing a style that produces trust." That remarkable young man was Jesus.

He went on to share with his followers not just some nice spiritual sayings but eight incredible insights on how good living and good leadership work. These ideas sounded strange. They seemed totally counterintuitive to the team.

In fact, Jesus' followers never really understood until he demonstrated the greatest act of humility, compassion, and commitment of all time: He gave his life for them.

Then he left. And without him around, these raw leadership recruits helped develop an organization that eventually changed the world.

That's why we believe these eight principles—known more commonly as the Beatitudes—are the keys to building trust with people. Putting them into practice will unlock your leadership potential and illumine the path to building a successful personal career and becoming a trusted leader of a team or organization.

To help you apply these principles more specifically to a leadership setting, we have taken a little liberty and restated the principles as follows:

1. *Humility:* "Favored are those not full of themselves"—leaders who are open and teachable…and invite the same qualities in others.
2. *Development:* "Favored are the realists"—leaders who accept the truth and know how to train others to seize the benefits of adversity, loss, and change.
3. *Commitment:* "Favored are the steadfast"—leaders who know that reaching a greater good requires a firm grip on the right values, causes, and goals.
4. *Focus:* "Favored are those desperate for excellence"—leaders who do the right things at the right time in the right way.
5. *Compassion:* "Favored are the caring"—leaders who serve the needs of everyone in their organizations.
6. *Integrity:* "Favored are those with unshakable ethics"—leaders who hold high moral values regardless of personal cost.
7. *Peacemaking:* "Favored are those who calm the waters"—leaders who remain steady in storms and build teams that stick together.
8. *Endurance:* "Favored are those with fortitude"—leaders who overcome personal doubts and setbacks to courageously stay the course.

We know that it may come as a bit of a shock to see Jesus' teachings applied in this context. But we need to understand his brilliance. He wasn't just an inspirational spiritual teacher. His timeless insights and the dynamic efforts and success of his followers mark Jesus as one of the greatest leaders of all time.

Few people consider themselves perfectly qualified to lead. The media—from ESPN to C-SPAN—tell us what everyone and everything should look like, and we find ourselves believing that skill is all that matters. We are even influenced by our own ideas about leadership. But Jesus had deeper insight and taught his followers that skill alone is not enough.

This book will guide you through the eight attributes of great leadership, with particular focus on the first and last: humility and endurance.

How to Get the Most from This Book

Our desire is to help you become a great leader. For the record, you do not have to be president of the United States or CEO of some international corporation to be a great leader. Just as parents don't suddenly decide to parent, leaders don't suddenly decide to lead. We are always leading. The important question is, "Just what kind of leader am I?"

To help make your time reading this book a pleasing and profitable investment, we have included two recurring sections at the end of each chapter to help you gain and retain as much wisdom as possible:

1. *The Essentials* provides a summary of the major ideas discussed in the chapter.
2. *Change from the Inside Out* includes questions and exercises to help you apply the chapter's material more specifically to yourself or to your team or organization.

Robert Quinn in his book *Deep Change* says, "We are all affected by technical competence or political acumen, but we are more deeply influenced by moral power. In the end, the latter is the ultimate source of power."[2]

The eight principles presented in this book will help you develop "the ultimate source of power" and create that successful, powerful, and *trusted* leadership style.

We invite you to explore the path that leads to trusted leadership. Together we can discover not just better leadership skills but, more important, better life skills.

Really, it can happen to you. *Trust us.*

"Favored Are Those Not Full of Themselves"

In a humble state, you learn better. I can't find anything else very exciting about humility, but at least there's that.

—JOHN DOONER, chairman and CEO of Interpublic,
as quoted in *Fast Company* magazine, November 2001

The pathway to greatness as a leader begins, ironically, with a step down. When Jesus took his ragtag group of twelve direct-reports on their mountainside leadership retreat, he began his training presentation (the Beatitudes) with the astonishing statement that "the poor in spirit" were the ones who would really make it big. And it's true. We have seen this over and over. It's not the loud, take-control, arrogant, hotshot "world beaters" who excel as leaders over the long term. No, the really great ones don't draw that much attention to themselves. They are, well, *humble.*

To many people, humility seems like a vice, weakness, or disease to avoid at all costs. Isn't a humble person a wimp or, worse, a cringing and despicable coward? Won't a humble leader be the object of contempt and abuse, the kind of person who gets trampled by all the aggressive ladder climbers in an organization?

This perception may have seemed accurate in the past, but not any longer. Jim Collins, author of the business book megaseller *Good to Great,* has this to say:

Level 5 leaders [individuals who blend extreme personal humility with intense professional will] channel their ego needs away from themselves and into the larger goal of building a great company. It's not that Level 5 leaders have no ego or self-interest. Indeed, they are incredibly ambitious—but their ambition is first and foremost for the institution, not themselves.[1]

Sounds a lot like humility, doesn't it?

Humility requires leaders to shed all their prejudices and biases. Humility requires you as a leader to examine who you are and what you have become. Humility requires a completely new way to evaluate people (and yourself). Just because individuals have made it to a higher position on the corporate ladder does not make them any smarter, any more correct in their decisions, or any more valuable than others within an organization. True humility leads to openness, teachability, and flexibility.

Much of the business world still believes that the take-charge, proud hero-leader is the answer to every company's prayers for a robust bottom line. This thinking may have made sense at one time, but no longer, as some of the world's largest companies have stumbled in shame under leadership styles that will never be described as humble.

So, can't an aggressive leader be effective? Of course. However, studies show when an aggressive leader (one lacking in humility) tries to force his or her own ideas on others, the rate of success is not as high as when the leader is open to new ideas and willing to listen, bend, change, and seek commitment from his or her people.

Pride focuses the attention of leaders onto themselves; humility focuses the attention of leaders onto others. The proud leader wants success that brings him perks. The humble leader wants success that brings enduring health to others and the organization. Which leader would you want to work for? Which one would you trust?

Humble leaders may not lead cheers for themselves, but neither are they retiring and shy people. These men and women stand firmly for their core beliefs and values. When you watch them work, their performance is graceful and smooth. They are a joy to talk to because they give no indication that they are an ounce more important than you are. Oh, and one more critical detail: These humble leaders produce incredible results.

Of course, there is more to being a trusted leader than having a humble attitude. That's why Jesus included an additional seven principles in that leadership seminar he gave over two thousand years ago. But the whole plan flows out of humility. Skip this one and you might as well forget about learning the other seven.

There's a bad-news/good-news aspect to the quality of humility. The bad news is that, to be honest, in the last fifteen years of consulting, we have encountered only a few truly humble leaders. If they were an animal species, they would definitely be on the endangered list. The good news is that, if you will learn how to humble yourself, the upside for you and your organization will be substantial. There isn't that much competition.

We urge you to put aside any pride and humble yourself to the first big idea of this book: The path to greatness begins with a step down to humility.

Feet on the Ground

We know it doesn't seem to make much sense, but the truly great leaders are humble.

The first problem comes with how the word is normally used: *Humble* is thought to mean shy, retiring, unobtrusive, quiet, unassuming. Being humble can seem weak or, horrors, even borrrrrrrriiiiiiiinnnnnngggggg.

So let's wipe the slate clean and make a fresh start with this word. *Humility* is derived from the Latin word *humus,* meaning "ground." One way to describe truly humble leaders is that they have their feet on the ground. Imagine for a moment a farmer in his field, sitting tall on his tractor, a wake of freshly turned earth foaming off the blade of his plow. He is sunburned. His arms are as sturdy as fence posts. He's a man of the *humus*—the earth. You could call him humble. Does this image suggest a lack of competence or strength? Do you sense it would be easy to take advantage of him? No, this image is one of strength and resilience. Think velvet-covered steel.

Humility is the first pillar of a leader whom others will trust.

A humble person sticks to the basics and is not prone to exaggeration. How much better off would we be today if the leaders of some of our fallen corporate behemoths had kept their heads out of the ozone and their feet on the ground?

Perhaps the most significant quality of humble leaders is their steady, clear-eyed perception of truth. A proud leader is prone to spreading and believing exaggerations—from little white lies to whopping falsehoods. Which high-powered modern leaders, intent on vanquishing foes and surmounting tall challenges, ever want to be known as humble? Not many—until, of course, they find out, as we intend to demonstrate, that humility is a critical first step on the path that leads to leadership success.

Why is humility such a key quality on a leader's personal résumé?

For starters, being humble prevents most of the mistakes that cripple a person who is proud. Consider Henry Ford, for example. He was an icon of American industry. His revolutionary ideas about manufacturing and design put him near the top of anyone's list of great American businessmen. Ford carried out his vision with the Model T. The car literally changed the face of America and the priorities of American citizens. By 1914, Henry Ford's factories built nearly 50 percent of all the cars sold in the United States. Now *that's* market share!

There was, however, a chink in Henry's armor. He was so proud of his Model T that he never wanted it to be changed or improved. One day, as the story goes, a group of his best engineers presented him with a new automobile design prototype. Ford became so angry that he pulled the doors right off the prototype and destroyed it with his bare hands.

Not until 1927 was Henry Ford willing to change to another model when, grudgingly, he allowed the Ford Motor Company to introduce the Model A. By that time, the company was well behind its competitors in design and technical advances. Ford's market share had plummeted to 28 percent by 1931.

Henry Ford just could not let go. He had created something, and he was unable to imagine that his "baby" could be improved. He was certain that he had the best ideas for "his" car. Nobody could help him, and he was unwilling to stretch himself to learn how he could make his product better or different.

At the same time, Ford undermined his executives, including his son Edsel.

As a result, he lost several key people to the competition. Apparently, Mr. Ford was not open to change—unless, of course, it was his idea. He succeeded in pulling down his management team and his company because he was so fixed upon his own ideas and methods. Consequently, he lost his executives, created havoc in his family, and damaged the company's market share beyond repair.

Henry Ford's leadership approach probably resembled what some now refer to as the hero-leader. Many organizations look to a hero-leader to deliver the power, charisma, ideas, and direction necessary to ensure a company's success. In many cases, the hero-leader does create blips in performance. For a time the dynamic chief is seen as a savior of the organization. *For a time.*

In an interview with *Fast Company* magazine, Peter Senge said,

Deep change comes only through real personal growth—through learning and unlearning. This is the kind of generative work that most executives are precluded from doing by the mechanical mind-set and by the cult of the hero-leader.[1]

Senge points out that the hero-leader approach is a pattern that makes it easier for companies to not change or move forward. The hero-leader weakens the organization and in many ways keeps it at an infant stage, very dependent upon the hero-leader's creativity and ideas. The people around the leader do not seek or promote change because the hero-leader is not open to new ideas (or ideas that he or she did not originate).

Under the hero-leader, people tend to acquiesce rather than work together as a team with a free exchange of ideas. The hero-leader may take the company in a new direction, but the troops within the organization only go along because it is a mandated change. This type of change is superficial at best.

Despite all of Henry Ford's incredible qualities, it sounds as if he was a proud rather than a humble leader. In his case, the Bible proverb certainly was true: "Pride leads to disgrace, but with humility comes wisdom."[2]

THE PITFALLS OF PRIDE

Before we paint the portrait of a humble leader, one who understands that he or she is not the center of anyone's universe and that other people have value and good ideas, let's make sure we understand the qualities of the opposite breed: a proud leader.

A proud leader is self-focused. For starters, an "unhumble" leader is notoriously self-focused. Writer and scholar Henri Nouwen once said, "It seems easier to be God than to love God, easier to control people than to love people." Isn't that the perception most people have? It is far easier (and seemingly satisfying) to be focused entirely on ourselves and not on the needs of others or the opportunities presented by others.

People who focus on themselves tend to create rigid rules and meaningless structure in order to protect what they perceive as a perfect environment.

One of the more popular episodes of the *Seinfeld* television series was the Soup Nazi. The story line centered on an aggressive man who owned a small restaurant where the locals stood outside in long lines to enjoy takeout orders of his delicious soup concoctions. However, these same customers were forced to tolerate this man's rigid rules: "Only one customer in the restaurant at a time." "Place your order immediately." "Do not point." "Do not ask questions." "Pay and leave immediately." Customers were forced to do what this man said, or they were told, "No soup for you! Come back in three months!"

Leaders with a Soup-Nazi style have one way of doing things—their way. Their focus is totally on themselves. They do not want (nor do they take) any suggestions. Their exact instructions are never to be questioned. They "know" what is best for the organization and everyone in it. They "allow" people to "help," but only under their carefully prepared set of rigid rules.

A proud leader is close minded. Don't confuse such a person with the facts. Close-minded leaders are not open to discussion and see no need to examine both sides of an issue. They know the truth and are usually its source. Anyone who dares to disagree with them is basically stupid. They take every measure to protect their point of view; they deny any effort to clarify the thought process; they do not encourage debate; they resist building a community of advisors.

A proud leader is critical. Such leaders develop self-centered standards and then tend to criticize anyone who does not follow their rules or who shows creativity and independence.

A few years ago we were advising the leadership team of a national toy retailer. During one of our visits in early December, two owners walked us through their distribution facility. The farther we walked, the more inventory we observed. The place was overflowing with toys. One owner saw what we saw and said with clenched jaw, his face reddening by the second, "You walk on without me. I need to talk to the warehouse manager."

He turned and ran to the warehouse manager's office. As we continued our tour of the facility, we heard this owner yelling at the top of his lungs at the warehouse manager, "Why is there so much stock in here? What are you doing to get this stuff out to the stores? It's Christmas, you know! Do you know what you're doing?"

Later we learned that the owner should have gathered a few facts before throwing a tantrum. He was so angry and intent on criticizing and assigning blame that he refused to listen to the warehouse manager's explanation. *Big mistake.* In reality, the warehouse was bulging because the Christmas sales cycle had not yet peaked. The warehouse manager was on his game. Trucks were running every day to local stores; the company had adopted a just-in-time inventory policy, and the manager was in fact responsible for the brilliant design and effective implementation of the program.

By the end of the holiday season, the toy retailer did achieve its sales and inventory targets. However, the owner's criticism of his warehouse manager caused permanent damage. The week after Christmas this top-quality manager resigned. Later he was asked to consider rejoining the organization, but he refused, saying, "I'm tired of being criticized at every turn. The owners ask us for input and help, yet they are so critical of our work. It's just not worth it."

A year later the Christmas season did not go as smoothly. The company tried to implement a new point-of-sale system, and it failed. You probably can guess why: The company lacked an experienced warehouse manager to help shape the back end of the system.

The Way of the Humble

Humble leaders take a different approach. They are not so self-absorbed as to think that they don't need to listen and be open. Their spirits are not critical because they are always open and scanning their employees, customers, and systems for new and better ideas. Following are some qualities of humble leaders.

A humble leader is teachable. Humble leaders never shut the door on educating themselves. They open themselves to the ideas and concepts of others—including their followers. A teachable leader enriches an organization and helps it stay ahead of the competition.

A teachable leader is open to personal and organizational change. This kind of leader is quick to understand that old routes are not always the best or the fastest. Conditions change. Memorizing approaches to problems, people, and cultures is much like carrying an old map—it goes out of date, and the traveler gets lost. Or the traveler is not aware of new streets that lead to better, more interesting destinations.

Recent research from the Center for Creative Leadership (CCL) shows that people can optimize their personal abilities as well as turbocharge their organization's adaptability and response to competitive challenges when they are committed to learning. According to researcher Ellen Van Velsor, "If things are going to continue to change, the one thing companies need above all else is people who have the ability to learn."

Monci Williams, in a *Harvard Management Update* article, provides several tips on being an effective and committed (active) learner:

1. *Take time to reflect.* Committed learners are "constantly devising rules about how things work (sense making). Rather than focusing solely on getting things done, they also pause to reflect."

2. *Tune in to the outside world.* Committed learners are not ingrown. "They constantly tune into the external world, making it a point to pick up what's going on around them."

3. *Regularly seek criticism.* Committed learners are "receptive to criticism" and "seek feedback regularly."

4. *Have a wide range of interests and move easily into new endeavors.* Committed learners are "perennially curious." They "indulge in a wide range of interests and pursuits (and enjoy various kinds of people), which prepares them for dealing with the unexpected when they encounter it. They will move easily into areas or endeavors that are not natural to them."

5. *Demonstrate an attitude of optimism and persistence.* Committed learners "are optimistic and persistent. They will try again and again—each time with a different tack—no matter how many times they fail."

6. *Learn from other people's failures and successes.* Committed learners "seek lessons in other people's failures and successes.... They learn from conversation...from books, watching movies, whatever is available."[3]

To be teachable, one must devote a significant amount of time to learning. *A humble leader is flexible.* An old proverb reminds us that "We cannot direct the wind, but we can adjust the sails." Many of us have spent our time trying to be in control, but a humble leader learns how to be effective without being in control. Humble leaders know that they cannot control people or circumstances. The irony is that the more they loosen their grip, the more they gain. The more flexibility—rather than control—that they can build into themselves, the more they succeed.

A humble leader welcomes change. Change often equals growth. But not change for the sake of change. A humble leader needs to discern the right change, a skill that is developed by being open and teachable.

Howard Hendricks, in his book *Teaching to Change Lives,* challenges leaders to embrace change:

> Write down somewhere in the margins on this page your answer to this question: How have you changed…lately? In the last week, let's say? Or the last month? The last year? Can you be very specific? Or must your answer be incredibly vague? You say you're growing. Okay…how? "Well," you say, "in all kinds of ways." Great! Name one.… The more you change, the more you become an instrument of change in the lives of others. If you want to become a change agent, you must also change.[4]

Why are so many leaders resistant to change and innovation?

1. They only want self-initiated change. Leaders who lack humility seek to develop only their own ideas. They have no interest in others' opinions.

2. They fear failure. We have seen so many potential leaders paralyzed by fear of failure. They fail to reach out for new territory because they are so afraid of losing. They do not understand the positive or learning side of failure.

Baseball star Barry Bonds strikes out more often than he hits home runs. However, Bonds keeps swinging for the fences. The best golfers in the world hit the green in regulation (two strokes under par) only about 75 percent of the time. One-fourth of the time they miss the mark. These golfers accept their failures, however, and give it their best to get back on track.

3. They are too comfortable. Many times present realities give us hope that we do not need to change. We sit in our current situations, do the same thing every day, and hold on for dear life to past achievements.

A leader willing to change brings about change in the organization.

Embracing change fosters an attitude of success and can deliver us from the quagmire of sameness.

Robert Quinn writes:

> Deep change requires more than the identification of the problem and a call for action. It requires looking beyond the scope of the problem and finding the actual source of the trouble. The real problem is frequently located where we would least expect to find it, inside ourselves. Deep change requires an evaluation of the ideologies behind the organizational culture. This process happens only when someone cares enough to exercise the courage to uncover the issues no one dares to recognize or confront. It means someone must be enormously secure and courageous. Culture change starts with personal change.[5]

Humble leaders are not afraid of personal change. They seek to improve themselves and their organizations. Change is the path to progress.

Humility leads to personal openness, teachability, and flexibility. Humility casts fears aside and frees leaders to energize and build their organizations toward common goals and vision. Humility is the fertile ground where the seeds of trust sprout.

THE ESSENTIALS

- Humility is the first pillar of a leader whom others will trust.
- The most significant quality of humble leaders is their steady, clear-eyed perception of truth.
- Being humble prevents most of the mistakes that cripple a person who is proud.

- In many cases the hero-leader does create blips in performance. For a time the dynamic chief is seen as a savior of the organization. *For a time.*
- The hero-leader weakens the organization and in many ways keeps it at an infant stage, very dependent upon the hero-leader's creativity and ideas. The people around the leader do not seek or promote change because the hero-leader is not open to new ideas (or ideas that he or she did not originate).
- The hero-leader may take the company in a new direction, but the troops within the organization only go along because it is a mandated change.

THE PITFALLS OF PRIDE

- The proud leader is self-focused.
- The proud leader is close minded.
- The proud leader is critical.

THE WAY OF THE HUMBLE

- A humble leader is teachable.
- A humble leader is flexible.
- A humble leader welcomes change.

CHANGE FROM THE INSIDE OUT

Being humble and teachable means learning to trust others and their opinions and instincts. It means listening with the intent of learning instead of simply responding. It means seeking personal development from every situation, experience (both good and bad), and transaction.

  - What in your life do you need to let go of so you can become more humble?

- Have you shared your vision with your colleagues? Have you asked them to participate? If not, why haven't you?
- Whom in your organization can you mentor—develop to his or her full potential?
- What can you do to improve your listening skills?

Finding Sparky

T his is not why leaders should want to be humble, but the truth is that humility pays big dividends in every relationship in an organization. For starters, a humble leader—one not caught up constantly in personal needs—is able to explore, develop, and encourage the strengths in others.

A humble leader wants to create a company of giants, to help people become "bigger" than they ever dreamed possible.

That's what this chapter is about…showing how humility absolutely fuels high staff morale and achievement in an organization. This is possible because the leader's ego isn't sucking all the air out of the creative environment. There is plenty of oxygen left over for others to breathe and make significant contributions.

And it's fun. Yes, it can be positively exhilarating to learn what qualities the creator has "hard-wired" into others. Many times a humble leader discovers strengths in his or her coworkers that even they have failed to detect. Sometimes you just don't know what precious gems are buried beneath the surface of another human being. We call this process "finding Sparky."

Say again? Let us explain with this story.

When he was a young boy, his friends gave him the nickname "Sparky" after a horse in the *Barney Google* comic strip. Though he was quite intelligent,

Sparky's shyness and timidity made school an agonizing experience. High school was especially challenging. He was a small, 136-pound pimply nobody. No one seemed to care about him. He remembered being astonished whenever anyone said hello. He had some skill in golf but lost an important match. He was a fair artist, but even the staff of his high-school yearbook would not publish his drawings. No one, including Sparky, seemed to think he had much to offer. He later said about this period in his life, "I never regarded myself as being much and I never regarded myself as being good-looking and I never had a date in high school, because I thought, who'd want to date me?"[1]

After high school he completed a correspondence course in art. He wrote a letter to Walt Disney Studios, hoping to be a cartoonist there. The studios requested drawings, and he worked many hours on them before mailing them to Disney. His reply from the studios: "rejected."

How did Sparky respond? He began drawing an autobiographical series of cartoons about a chronic underachiever, a boy whose kite would never fly. It wasn't that long before the whole world became acquainted with this character named Charlie Brown—as well as friends of his named Lucy, Linus, Pig Pen, and Snoopy. Sparky—Charles Schulz—became the most famous and wealthy cartoonist ever. At the height of his popularity, his cartoon strip *Peanuts* appeared in 2,600 papers in twenty-one languages in seventy-five countries. In 1978 he was named International Cartoonist of the Year.[2] The whole *Peanuts* cartoon gang once appeared on a cover of *Time* magazine. This "loser" in high school really had some potential after all.

A humble leader is always looking for Sparkies.

Each person with whom a leader works has hidden gifts and talents, and someone may even have the enormous potential of a Sparky. We need to help them uncover, develop, and use those talents. Humble leaders relish the idea of helping people find their unique niche. They enjoy moving people along to bigger and better things. They celebrate the victories and provide encouragement when their people are discouraged or fearful of moving ahead.

Take Gary, for example. He worked in the mailroom for one of our clients. Unknown to his employer, Gary was a computer genius. When the president of the company needed help, we suggested Gary, and he delivered. Today, Gary is a highly respected computer executive. He got his start from an executive who was open and humble.

Many leaders focus on people's weaknesses. They are always trying to "fix" someone. They fail to recognize potential and help people develop a path for personal success and reward.

FOCUS ON WHAT PEOPLE CAN BECOME

One way to exhibit humility and move away from the trap of self-oriented leadership is to focus on what people can become. This requires shifting away from criticizing how staff members are doing to celebrating how far they have come in improving their performance. If this concept seems hard to grasp, just apply it to yourself and think about what motivates you to do better—a tongue lashing or a pat on the back?

Have you ever watched how parents behave while teaching their children to walk? Little Sally first pulls herself to a wobbly, standing position by grabbing a chair or table leg. The parents go crazy—all kinds of applause, yells of approval, and generous words like "Good job!" Mom and Dad do not expect darling Sal to run at this point; that would be ludicrous. But they urge her to try to walk. With such encouragement, Sally thinks she can conquer the world. She tries a tentative step and falls in a heap. Cheers and applause rain down.

Now really full of confidence, the tot takes two steps before crashing. This triggers an Olympic medal–winning response. Telephone calls are made to grandparents, and video cameras roll. Over the next few weeks, Sally takes several steps, falls down with even greater flourish, gets up, and takes several more steps. Her parents celebrate every move. Sally conquers her world.

Fast-forward ten-plus years. Sally is now a teenager. She wants more space;

she wants to make more and more of her own decisions. She's a good kid but not perfect. She's learning to drive but hits the curb repeatedly. Are her parents celebrating? No. Actually they are pretty annoyed. *Shouldn't she know better? Is she just being rebellious?* Instead of remembering that Sally is learning and cheering how far their child has come ("Wow! She only hits curbs on the right-hand side of the street now!"), they hone in on today's mistakes. Instead of celebrating small victories as they did years ago when Sally was a world-class novice walker, her parents yell and criticize. And guess what? Sally is discouraged. Her confidence is shaken—*Maybe I will never be a decent driver.* And to top it off, she's mad at Mom and Dad.

Allow this illustration to sink deeply into your grid as you consider how to relate to subordinates. *Work very hard at praising progress instead of emphasizing error.*

Every human being has greatness inside. There are no exceptions. Humble leaders look for and honor this greatness in people. They see people as able to grow and contribute. They see people for what they can become.

Every year the NFL draft illustrates this principle. Scouts compile detailed reports on college football players for teams and coaches. Film is run and rerun. Players are tested for physical, mental, and emotional strength. Then, on draft day choices are made. In the first round or two, the can't-miss stars are picked. What's really interesting, though, are the picks made in later rounds.

Bart Starr, former quarterback of the Green Bay Packers, was a second-stringer in college. The Packers, seeing something in Starr that others had missed, picked him very late in the draft. Under legendary coach Vince Lombardi, Starr later led the Packers to five world championships. He was the starting quarterback in the first two Super Bowls. Long before anyone else believed in Starr's ability, Lombardi saw his potential greatness.

Humble leaders look for the potential in others and do everything they can to develop it. Have you ever tried to drive your car with the parking brake on? There the Porsche sits, engine revving, but it is not able to peel away at full speed. That is exactly what happens when leaders do not develop the potential of other people. They forget to release the brake.

UNLEASHING GREATNESS IN OTHERS

A humble leader steps aside so that others can run by and seize the prize of their own greatness. But just how is this done? Here's an overview:

Assume the best of others. Leaders who expect the best of others exert a powerful influence. Many times leaders get caught in the trap of judging others. They measure, categorize, and classify people and the jobs they perform. Ken Blanchard likes to talk about "catching people doing things right." This idea puts the emphasis on solid behavior and good intentions. It forces managers to assume and reward the best. It helps leaders not make rigid rules that hold down employees who want to soar.

Learn to listen. The apostle James, a great follower of Jesus, wrote, "My dear brothers and sisters, be quick to listen, slow to speak, and slow to get angry."[3] Being quick to listen implies that a leader is paying attention, that he or she is not distracted but is actively hearing what the other person is saying. A humble leader listens with the intent of understanding rather than responding.

Reward honest communication. How do you react when someone tells you bad news? Does the messenger become a target for your arrows? We know a man who confronted his boss over a matter that had the potential to really upset the company's applecart. Instead of shooting the messenger, the supervisor commended the truth-bearer for his straightforward approach and creativity. He was able to look past the message to the employee's intentions. The boss agreed with his employee in significant ways and changed his perspective. He rewarded open communication, and the company was better off because of it.

Admit your mistakes. Humble, open leaders show vulnerability. And nothing demonstrates vulnerability quite like admitting mistakes. "I was wrong" is difficult to say, but it is one of the most freeing and powerful statements a leader can make. Admitting your mistakes allows others on the team to relax and admit their mistakes. It allows the team to breathe and grow. Admission of wrong, seeking and granting forgiveness, and moving on are powerful tools of a humble leader.

Commit to developing others. Developing others first takes personal commitment and desire. It means taking the time to know people—their preferences, skills, and goals. This is most often accomplished in personal relationships.

Share the dream. Leaders often make the mistake of not being open or sharing their vision and goals with their people. Your vision is not something to hide. Sharing it with others helps them understand what they need to contribute. You can then develop their potential around a shared vision.

Seek commitment. Once people understand your goals and you begin to understand their needs and potential, you can then seek their commitment. Ken Blanchard draws a line between people who are "just interested" and those who are committed. He often relates this well-known story:

A chicken and a pig were walking down the street one day and noticed some poor children who looked as if they hadn't eaten anything for days. Moved with compassion, the chicken said to the pig, "I have an idea! Let's give those children a nice breakfast of ham and eggs." The pig contemplated the chicken's suggestion and said, "Well, for you, that would involve a small sacrifice; but for me, it would involve total commitment!"[4]

Good leaders understand the need to develop committed people.

Set goals. Developing people's potential (and then being open to their ideas) involves setting mutually agreed-upon goals. Individuals also need to know whether they are meeting the standard.

Reward and recognize. In addition to setting goals, it is important to make people feel appreciated. What reward systems can be implemented to help people feel they have contributed? Money simply levels the playing field. Employees believe you are simply providing fair compensation for their additional efforts; therefore, money pays only for what they have already given. Discovering and supporting an employee's Growth Achievement Path (GAP) does so much more for morale than money—and much more than leveling the playing field.

Let's go back to the story about Gary, the mailroom clerk. He worked hard and was a well-liked employee, but nobody ever thought much about him. Gary could walk in and out of a room and hardly anyone would notice. He was just delivering the mail. But Gary had a different image of himself. He loved computers. He was taking the time and effort to learn how they ran and what he could accomplish with them. Gary would not grow or experience a sense of achievement as a mailroom clerk, but he would as a computer expert. His GAP was to pursue a career that would bring him satisfaction and give him opportunities to grow and achieve—to be someone in demand, someone who would be respected and noticed when he walked into a room. His GAP was very different from his current circumstances.

When we suggested to the president that he first look to Gary for help rather than hire a computer expert out of house, he was skeptical. But when he decided to talk to Gary, Gary was so enthusiastic that the president decided to give it a shot.

There has never been a more dedicated employee than Gary. He went well above and beyond the call of duty to make sure the company's computer system performed to a high level and was ready to meet any of the company's demands. Gary was given a position that aligned with his GAP.

Employees usually fall into one of four GAP categories:

1. *No GAP.* Some employees have no idea what kind of work would get their passion and juices flowing. To them, work is just work; it does nothing to satisfy needs for growth and achievement. In fact, the no-GAP crowd doesn't appear to be interested in growth or achievement but seems to find satisfaction in self-indulgent pursuits such as drinking, sports, or other self-focused activities. The no-GAP crowd

is almost impossible to motivate and should be the first considered when corporate cuts are made.

2. *Outside GAP.* In some cases, people will most definitely be motivated by avenues outside of their jobs. Maybe their GAP is in charity work of one sort or another that will never provide financial security, so their efforts are focused on following their GAP through outside interests. These people are motivated by highly secure and reasonably well-paying jobs that enable them to pursue their outside GAP. They can be very highly motivated and perform very well in their jobs if they find reward and satisfaction in outside interests.

3. *Undiscovered GAP.* This is a tough category because these people are not self-reflective enough to know that they have or should have a GAP. They can become very motivated if they discover their GAP, but it takes a lot of energy on the part of a leader to help them reach this point.

4. *Known GAP.* A good number of people know or at least sense what their GAP is. However, they can often get trapped doing what they are good at, or they may find that their organization keeps them locked in a specific box and doesn't allow them to pursue their GAP. If these people are allowed to pursue their GAP, they often become the most motivated and high-performance persons on a team.

Some wonderful studies have been conducted to discover what really motivates people. One of the findings is that anytime money is involved, the actual impact on motivation is quite different from what might be assumed.

Companies and leaders often believe that money is the best way to really reward and motivate employees for outstanding performance. Of course money is always appreciated and normal merit increases and bonuses should be given. But many employees feel after an extraordinary performance that they have already given the company a valuable effort and a financial payment only "levels the playing field"—in effect, it is just fair, additional compensation for above-and-beyond-the-call achievement.

It is much more meaningful and satisfying (and ultimately *motivating*) to be rewarded according to your GAP. It's important that you as a leader understand the GAP of the people who are working for you. As with Gary, some employees may be motivated by a different kind of work. Others may prefer having more time off to focus on being a better dad or mom. Or maybe someone has an entrepreneurial spirit that needs to be unleashed.

We know a software-company president who hired a programmer who is not only extremely talented but also suggested significant changes to the software that led to better customer satisfaction and higher sales. This guy deserved a significant reward. The president discovered that the programmer was an excellent guitar player but had never owned a good guitar. The president gave him a highly rated (and expensive) guitar as a gift. Extra money would have been appreciated, but this president made a huge motivational impact because he understood his employee's GAP. The employee was thrilled with both the gift and the thought and understanding of the president that engendered it.

Allow for midcourse corrections. Do not be rigid in your planning with people. Invariably, changes in market conditions, employee needs, and other factors will alter plans and goals. That's life; that's okay. Developing someone's potential is not a fixed proposition but rather a fluid system that responds to his or her needs and skills as well as your needs and vision.

The Sweet Rewards

Humility is costly, but there are incredible and often surprising rewards for leaders who recognize their own personal strengths and limitations while seeing and encouraging the greatness in others. Sometimes the ramifications of this timeless insight bring a smile.

Imagine a traditional, buttoned-down, classy department store with the expected crew of nicely dressed, decorous department managers and floor

35

workers. In the midst of this stable setting appears a freewheeling bohemian hippie throwback with an attitude!

While consulting with a large department store chain, we encountered such a situation with a particular store employee. The management team just did not respect this guy because he did not fit the mold of the "perfect" floor salesperson. He dressed way too casually (did he even own a tie?). He wore his hair very long. His humor was caustic. He talked too loudly and joked too much. The only thing standing between him and a pink slip was the small matter of *performance*. He was positively brilliant at what he did!

His specialty was the children's clothing department where the kids (and moms) loved him. To them, he was a funny, warm, and highly entertaining friend, a trusted advisor in selecting the best things to wear. Because the customers understood this man's intentions—he loved meeting kids on their level and serving them—his countercultural appearance and behavior didn't matter much. As long as his creative approach and personality accomplished the mission, he deserved to be a hero of management, not a personnel headache.

This man definitely was a Sparky.

Sure, this example may be a bit extreme, but it illustrates the principle beautifully: A humble leader, who is not too full of self, has the capacity and good sense to allow others to sparkle and make a difference.

THE ESSENTIALS

- Many times a humble leader discovers strengths in his or her coworkers that even they have failed to detect.
- Humble leaders relish the idea of helping people find their unique niche. They enjoy moving people along to bigger and better things. They cele-

brate the victories and provide encouragement when their people are discouraged or fearful of moving ahead.

Focus on What People Can Become

- One way to exhibit humility and move away from the trap of self-oriented leadership is to focus on what people can become.
- Celebrate how far people have come in improving their performance.
- Work very hard at praising progress instead of emphasizing error.
- Every human being has greatness inside. Humble leaders look for and honor this greatness in people.

Unleashing Greatness in Others

- Assume the best of others.
- Learn to listen.
- Reward honest communication.
- Admit your mistakes.
- Commit to developing others.
- Share the dream.
- Seek commitment.
- Set goals.
- Reward and recognize.
- Allow midcourse corrections.

The Sweet Rewards

- A humble leader, who is not too full of self, has the capacity and good sense to allow others to sparkle and make a difference.

CHANGE FROM THE INSIDE OUT

Overcontrol diminishes trust. Control-freak leaders have a hard time building truly great teams. Their lack of trust in subordinates hamstrings creativity and superior performance. Give yourself this quiz:

- On a scale of 1 to 5, rate your need for control in various situations.
- Are you open to other people's ideas, creativity, advice, and vision? Why or why not?
- What can you do today to be more flexible as you work with subordinates? How could you encourage their ideas, creativity, and vision?
- Do you enjoy learning? Do you have a willingness to try new things? If not, why not?
- What steps can you take to create a climate for change in your company?
- Have you gotten to know your subordinates well enough to know their Growth Achievement Potential? What are you doing to motivate people according to their GAP?

"Favored Are the Realists"

Management's imperative is to cultivate its human resources.

—ZIG ZIGLAR, *Top Performance*

L eaders are defined by those who follow them. If they cannot or choose not to develop others, chances are good they will not be leaders for long.

We have seen how personal humility establishes a healthy foundation in a leader's outlook. Now we need to develop the right qualities in ourselves and others.

C. William Pollard, chairman of the board at ServiceMaster, relates how he and his team finally grasped this principle:

Several years ago the ServiceMaster board of directors had a two-day session with Peter Drucker. The purpose of our time was to review how we could be more effective in our planning and governance. Peter started off the seminar with one of his famous questions: "What is your business?" The responses were varied and included the identification of markets we serve, such as our health care, education, and residential; and the services we deliver, such as food service, housekeeping, and maid service.

After about five minutes of listening to the responses regarding our markets and services, Peter told our board something that I have never been able to tell them. He said, "You are all wrong. Your business is simply the training and development of people. You package it all different ways to meet the needs and demands of the customer, but your basic business is people training and motivation. You are delivering services. You can't deliver services without people. You can't deliver quality service to the customer without motivated and trained people."[1]

Development, the second attribute of a trustworthy leader, requires a humble attitude and a long-term commitment to growth and improvement. Benjamin Franklin once said, "You can't expect an empty bag to stand up straight." Neither can leaders expect people to grow, achieve goals, and improve the organization without investing the time necessary to develop them into top performers and men and women of character.

As you will see repeatedly in this book, however, growth must first take place in leaders' lives. There are some attitudes and habits close to home that must be cleaned up. Jesus once said, "Why do you look at the speck of sawdust in your brother's eye and pay no attention to the plank in your own eye?"[2] What he meant, of course, is that some strenuous self-examination is always a good first step in determining truth.

After we let go of a few personal "planks" and seek to understand the reality of the environment where we lead, we will then be ready to powerfully develop others.

4

Letting Go

eveloping your own untapped and unrefined potential is a bit like remodeling an old house: First, you have to tear out some things— like pride or extreme self-sufficiency or bullheadedness or trying to overcontrol people or _____ (fill in the blank with some attitude or behavior of yours that makes you say "ouch!").

An experience of mine (Wayne's) helps illustrate how certain personal qualities can trip us up: A few years ago I was in Greenville, South Carolina, visiting some retail operations. Before heading for my next stop in Waynesboro, North Carolina, I asked the man I was with for the best route.

"Take the interstate north until you hit such and such a highway, and drive straight west. That's the way you want to go."

As he talked I was glancing at my map and noticed another route that appeared more direct. "What about this road?" I asked. "It looks like a more direct route."

"You can get there that way, but I wouldn't suggest it."

So guess which road I took? I thought I knew a good idea when I saw it— and isn't a straight line the shortest distance between two points?

Well, if I could have driven in a straight line across all those mountains,

I would have been pleased with my choice! But this was about the curviest road you could find. I have never driven so many hours in first gear. My appointment was for two o'clock in the afternoon, and I probably would have made it by taking the longer route. But when I rolled in at 5 P.M., horribly embarrassed—my hands clawlike after gripping the steering wheel that long—I was a more humble man.

That particular day it would have been good if I had let go of a crippling misperception of reality.

Letting go will often appear counterintuitive. Let's imagine you are grasping a rope that is dangling you from a window of a three-story house, which happens to be on fire. Hanging on for your life makes sense only until the firemen come and are stationed below to catch you. Now it makes sense to let go.

We agree that many leaders would rather get and keep a grip than lose their grip. But if you want to build trust with others, you need to have the ability to let go. The discussion here is not about delegation. It concerns letting go of personal qualities that build walls not only between you and your team but also within yourself.

LETTING GO OF BAD ATTITUDES

If you want to grab hold of the eight energizing, productive principles we advocate in this book, you must first let go of some bad attitudes.

Pride

Pride is pure selfishness. A proud leader's mind is closed to new truths; he or she is unteachable. Pride causes inflexibility: "We will only pursue my ideas, thank you very much." Pride resists change. Pride forces us to care more about status and prestige. Pride gets in the way of asking others for help.

Pride is a focus on us rather than on the development of other people.

Pride causes a destructive competition between our team members and us, and between their ideas and ours. Pride says, "I have to win." It forces us to fight for *our* ideas and *our* ways just for the sake of winning the argument, not for the development of the organization or other people. As an old saying goes, "An egotist is a man whose self-importance makes his mind shrink while his head swells."

The opposite of pride is humility. Humility is self-effacement rather than self-advertisement. It focuses our attention away from ourselves and onto other people and their development. It involves being flexible enough to listen and be taught by others. It means allowing other people to generate new ideas and supporting those ideas even if they fail. It is realizing that the whole team, organization, or business unit is not dependent solely on you.

Pride is a wall; humility is a gate.

Ego defines your boundaries of influence. A large ego is like a tall cylinder, very high and visible, but the boundaries of influence are not very expansive. However, a small ego is like a low but wide cylinder. Its boundaries of influence reach much farther than that of a big ego.

A Judgmental Attitude

Another bad attitude leaders must rid themselves of is a judgmental attitude toward others—"Stop judging others, and you will not be judged. For others will treat you as you treat them. Whatever measure you use in judging others, it will be used to measure how you are judged."[1]

Jesus' statement is against the kind of hypocritical, judgmental attitude that tears others down in order to build oneself up. It is not a blanket statement against all critical thinking, but a call to be *discerning* rather than negative.

Judgmental leaders are negative and critical. Inside they may be angry or suffering from insecurity and low self-esteem. The result of this kind of attitude is a group of employees and team members who are afraid to act.

The judgmental leader needs to learn to become a developer, a builder. To fulfill this role, the leader needs to behave nonjudgmentally. In order to do that, he or she must respect, understand, accept, believe, and hope in subordinates and all team members.

Uncontrolled Will

An uncontrolled will is a negative force that is rooted in a deep stubbornness and an attachment to personal (and immediate) gratification, mostly at the cost of the development of others. Leaders with uncontrolled wills avoid committing to common values or ideals beyond their own. Rather than a stubborn will, we need a focused will that centers on development, goals, and productivity.

In the 1960s a study was conducted with four-year-old children. In the experiment the children were each brought into a room, and on the table in front of them was a marshmallow treat. The facilitator explained that he or she must leave for a moment. During the facilitator's absence, the child had the choice of either eating one marshmallow or waiting until the facilitator returned to get two marshmallows. As you can imagine, some of the children waited not even a few seconds before consuming the one marshmallow. There were no consequences; they were just not offered a second marshmallow. The other children used whatever means possible to delay their gratification until the facilitator returned so they would receive the additional marshmallow.

The study was completed twelve to fourteen years later when these former four-year-olds were now seniors in high school. Researchers found a strong correlation between the children's initial ability to delay gratification and how well they were functioning as young adults in society. Those who had been unable to delay their gratification as four-year-olds now had trouble functioning socially and emotionally; they tended to be easily frustrated, mistrustful of others, and temperamental. And they were still unable to delay their own gratification. Members of the group that had done whatever it took to wait for the additional treat were top performers, able to conduct themselves well in almost any setting. They had also retained their ability to delay gratification in order to achieve their goals.[2]

Keeping our egos in check and our wills under control enables us to function much better as teammates and leaders.

Allowing Ourselves to Stagnate

Leaders who allow themselves to stagnate become apathetic or purposeless, and their attention is scattered. Stagnation also ushers in uncontrolled thoughts and can be a foundation for laziness.

Frustration, burnout, and self-will can often cause stagnation. Likewise, when we feel overlooked or feel that our work doesn't quite measure up, we have a tendency to sit back and let someone else take over. Stagnation also develops from not being asked to contribute. When leaders take control of innovation, followers can simply give up because their input is not wanted or appreciated.

Common traits that lead to stagnation are perfectionism or mistaking activity for achievement. Leaders who are perfectionistic or are more focused on activity than achievement create a stagnant work force. People give up trying to achieve anything meaningful because the perfectionistic leader never appreciates their achievements but rather picks apart everything they do. Or the activity-driven leader will see a coworker as lazy if he or she completes a project a half-day early and then uses the saved hours for some downtime.

Rather than allowing themselves to stagnate, leaders need to serve and teach boldly and provide vision, goals, and assistance to subordinates and team members.

Insensitivity

Insensitive leaders are unconcerned about others. They have no empathy and are uncaring. They do not listen—not because they are prideful but because they lack compassion. They are so hardened that they can unknowingly hurt people and kill ideas and creativity.

Compassion, on the other hand, develops as a result of treating your neighbor as yourself. It involves serving your employees, team members, and customers with empathy. It means taking the time to understand coworkers and team members. It involves genuine listening.

Dishonesty

Dishonesty involves more than cheating, lying, or stealing; it is rooted in deceit. Dishonesty happens when a leader denies reality or seeks gain through deviousness. It is about game playing, manipulation, and pretense.

We once worked with a member of an executive team in a large international corporation. Known for his consistently high performance, Todd had been promoted to lead the rescue of one of the corporation's failing divisions in another country.

As Todd began to work his "magic" on his new division, the numbers slowly improved. After several quarters this division's performance had reached an acceptable level. Everyone up the line was happy, that is until some disturbing signals surfaced.

People who worked in Todd's division began to talk about whether they were on his team or not. If you were a "team player" for Todd, it seemed you could do nothing wrong. But if you were not on Todd's team, there was almost no way to get out of the doghouse.

At the same time, at the executive leadership level, signs of mistrust were developing between Todd and his peers. People were becoming guarded about what they said and what they believed about what was being said. Teamwork was breaking down.

When the situation was described to the CEO and the opinion was offered that maybe Todd was not a good fit for the position, the CEO would hear nothing of it. Todd's performance was just too good. How could the CEO take action against Todd simply because there was a little "jealousy" on the team?

Nearly a year later the situation at the leadership level had deteriorated to the point that many team members were threatening to quit because there was so little trust. They felt they had to protect their backs at all times. At that time we conducted a coaching session on revealing the core competencies of individuals, and Todd was described as Machiavellian. The interesting thing was that Todd didn't seem offended by this description and, in fact, quite agreed with it. As it turned out, Todd had been trained in both union and hostage negotiation and believed that the ends always justified the means. For him, it was perfectly normal and moral to say whatever it took to accomplish the goal. He was quite surprised when the leadership team felt they could not work with him any longer because of his dishonesty.

It took another year before the CEO finally came to grips with the situation and asked Todd to move on. Following his departure everyone was astounded at the depth of destruction he had caused in the company (in spite of his solid financial performance). Leadership had been decimated. The division's performance collapsed to a true level, not the propped-up levels. Recovery took several years.

Dishonesty always destroys the fiber of a company—regardless of how good the numbers are.

The scandal at Enron also illustrates the bitter fruit of dishonesty. The numbers were manipulated to tell investors the wrong story. This dishonest practice led to the downfall of an organization, and the results are still being felt. Also, a nationally recognized accounting firm ended up in shambles, and employees' retirement funds are gone, all because of manipulation and deceit.

Integrity overcomes dishonesty. Leaders of integrity strive to avoid the deceitfulness of appearances. They are genuine, sincere, authentic, and trust-worthy—qualities that build the confidence of coworkers and employees in their leaders.

Divisiveness

Nothing can destroy a team or an organization like a divisive leader. Fear, anxiety, and confusion rip apart relationships and teams. Shared vision and values are trashed. Divisiveness can create an us-versus-them atmosphere that separates workers from management, management from executives, and executives from the board. It literally is war.

Great leaders build great teams where the level of trust and mutual respect is so high that team members can openly, and even strongly, disagree with one another and then work toward effective solutions. Confrontational behavior enables team members to fully explore and understand the differences. Then everyone knows that each point of view has received full consideration before a decision is reached.

Avoidance of Suffering

Leaders who avoid suffering always choose the easiest solution or decision. They avoid problems, responsibilities, and difficulties. They lack perseverance, endurance, and courage. They have lost the will to grow.

Avoidance also leads to a focus on the short term. Leaders who are "avoiders" make decisions that take away the short-term pain without regard for the benefits to be gained from longer-term struggles. They avoid trouble today without regard for the future, and as a result, their people are always scrambling to keep things together. Leaders who choose avoidance completely miss out on the opportunity to grow through adversity.

Instead of choosing to avoid suffering, leaders who persevere will gain experiential knowledge and confidence. These valuable qualities can be passed along to benefit others in the organization as well.

That's quite a list! Just think how your quality of life will improve (it won't happen overnight) if you loosen your grip and let go of each of these bad attitudes. You will increasingly be a leader of influence whom others will trust and follow.

LETTING GO OF A BAD IDEA

There is something else a growing leader must let go of that's so important we've assigned it a category of its own. It is the enormously flawed idea that in making your way through life *only success is of any value.*

The truth is that one of the most "successful" things you can ever learn is how to profit from a good failure. Let's face it, reality teaches us that failure is inevitable. Since this is the case, we had better learn how to accept failure and make the most of it.

Everybody makes mistakes, including great leaders. Nobody—repeat, nobody—normally gets it right the first time. (Most of us don't get it right the second, third, or fourth times either!) Winston Churchill said it best: "Success is the ability to go from failure to failure without losing your enthusiasm." This was born out in Churchill's own life and in his political career in Great Britain when he blew one assignment after another. Finally, as prime minister during World War II, he faced the greatest leadership challenge of his career as he tried to hold together a struggling nation under the constant threat of bombings, lack of provisions, and fear. Having learned from past mistakes, he rose to the challenge and saved his country.

Consider the record of several successful people who maintained great enthusiasm while failing repeatedly:

- Babe Ruth struck out 1,330 times. He also hit 714 home runs.

- R. H. Macy failed in the retail business before he got it right with his department store in New York City.
- Abraham Lincoln failed twice in business and was defeated in six state and national elections before winning the presidency.
- Theodor S. Geisel (Dr. Seuss) had his first children's book rejected by twenty-three publishers in a row. The twenty-fourth accepted the manuscript, and it sold six million copies.[3]

Why is it that with all that is written about the benefit of failure so many leaders struggle to allow their people or organizations to "fail successfully"? The following reasons have been given at one time or another.

"It has to be somebody's fault." Many organizations fear failure and make attempts to cover up mistakes or failed initiatives. To compensate for their fears, leaders often create a culture of blame. Something goes wrong, and immediately the leadership looks for someone or something to blame. Nobody takes personal responsibility; it's much easier to find someone to blame. We see this everywhere—in large corporations, small businesses, charitable organizations, government agencies, even in churches. If there is a problem, a scapegoat must be found to bear the blame.

Perhaps the most widely embraced delusion in business today is that it's possible and even desirable to create organizations in which mistakes are rare rather than a necessary cost of doing business. The problem with embracing this fantasy is that it encourages you and your associates to hide mistakes, shift the blame for them, or pretend they don't exist for as long as you possibly can.

"Small mistakes are great learning opportunities," says Dennis Matthies, a Bellevue, Washington–based learning consultant. "They show 'cracks'—areas of vulnerability—where you don't pay the price now but might later."

"We expect perfection." Although most leaders certainly grasp the possibility if not the inevitability of failure, they still don't like the concept. In their hearts they simply cannot tolerate anything but an absolute zero-defects mentality.

They really seem to believe that if their people *really* try they will not fail. The leaders are either embarrassed by failure, too proud to admit failure, or do not want the "mess" that some failures can cause.

Whatever the root cause of such an executive mind-set may be, it creates crushing, unrealistic expectations for leaders and their employees.

Tom Peters advances a more sane approach:

The goal is to be more tolerant of slip-ups. You must be like [Les] Wexner [Limited founder] and actively encourage failure. Talk it up. Laugh about it. Go around the table at a project group meeting or morning staff meeting: Start with your own most interesting foul-up. Then have everyone follow suit. What mistakes did you make this week? What were the most interesting ones? How can we help you make more mistakes, faster?…Look to catch someone doing something wrong![4]

Rather than setting unrealistic expectations, leaders should expect people to fail and be ready to forgive and move on. Leaders can help an organization learn from its mistakes and push ahead to new innovation and creativity. This idea has been referred to as "failing forward." People learn from each failure, and the lessons learned are quickly channeled into modifying the plan, design, or strategy.

One of our executive clients is especially good at learning from failure. This man never seems to be interested in who is at fault but is simply interested in what the current situation is and how to move ahead. That keeps the situation positive as well as focused on learning and making improvements. The person who made the mistake or failed is not forgotten but is mentored and developed for future growth. Or at times the person who failed is assisted in finding another job elsewhere in the company or even with another firm where there's a better chance for personal success. But the failure is always seen by this effective executive as a learning opportunity rather than an occasion to assign blame.

The irony is that seeking perfection and setting ridiculously high expectations is almost a guaranteed means of lowering performance. It makes everybody uptight. And people "playing tight" are mistake-prone. Failing may become the norm.

You don't want yourself or others to become dispirited, unable to create or innovate because something deep inside whispers, "What's the use? I'll fail anyway." The way out of this trap is to win some small victories so that confidence returns. Small successes, as they accumulate, can morph into large victories and help restore individual and team trust.

"We've always done it this way." Some leaders are stuck in the past. They may have won big "back in '89," and now that shining moment is enshrined in their mental hall of fame. A huge past mistake can have the same result; leaders no longer trust their judgment and can't move ahead boldly.

Rather than dwelling on past mistakes, leaders need to use those experiences to create new and different solutions.

Do yourself a favor and don't just become acquainted with failure: Make it your friend.

GET A GRIP—LET GO!

Every leader is constantly making choices. Is there a way to make more correct turns at each crossroads we encounter instead of taking long, circuitous routes that cost us time and productivity?

Of course the answer is yes. In fact, once you grasp the concept of letting go, you will be well on your way to successfully developing great qualities in yourself and others.

THE ESSENTIALS

- Leaders are defined by those who follow them.
- Development requires a humble attitude and a long-term commitment to growth and improvement.
- Growth must first take place in leaders' lives. There are some attitudes and habits close to home that must be cleaned up.
- Letting go will often appear counterintuitive.
- If you want to build trust with others, you need to have the ability to let go.

Letting Go of Bad Attitudes

- *Pride*—A proud leader's mind is closed to new truths; he or she is unteachable. The opposite of pride is humility. It focuses our attention away from ourselves and onto other people and their development.
- *A judgmental attitude*—A judgmental attitude tears others down in order to build oneself up. The developer must respect, understand, accept, believe, and hope in subordinates and all team members.
- *Uncontrolled will*—Leaders with uncontrolled wills avoid committing to common values or ideals beyond their own. Rather than a stubborn will, we need a focused will that centers on development, goals, and productivity.
- *Allowing ourselves to stagnate*—Leaders who allow themselves to stagnate become apathetic or purposeless, and their attention is scattered. Rather than allowing themselves to stagnate, leaders need to serve and teach boldly and provide vision, goals, and assistance to subordinates and team members.

- *Insensitivity*—Insensitive leaders are so hardened that they can unknowingly hurt people and kill ideas and creativity. Compassionate leaders take the time to understand coworkers and team members.
- *Dishonesty*—This happens when a leader denies reality or seeks gain through deviousness. Integrity overcomes dishonesty.
- *Divisiveness*—Divisiveness can create an us-versus-them atmosphere that separates workers from management, management from executives, and executives from the board. It literally is war. Great leaders build great teams where the level of trust and mutual respect is so high that team members can openly, and even strongly, disagree with one another and then work toward effective solutions.
- *Avoidance of suffering*—Leaders who avoid suffering always choose the easiest solution or decision. Leaders who persevere will gain experiential knowledge and confidence.

Letting Go of a Bad Idea

- The truth is that one of the most "successful" things you can ever learn is how to profit from a good failure.
- Everybody makes mistakes.
- Organizations that fear failure often compensate for those fears by creating a culture of blame.
- "Small mistakes are great learning opportunities."
- Some leaders simply cannot tolerate anything but an absolute zero-defects mentality. They are either embarrassed by failure, too proud to admit failure, or do not want the "mess" that some failures can cause.
- The irony is that seeking perfection and setting ridiculously high expectations is almost a guaranteed means of lowering performance.
- Some leaders are stuck in the past. Rather than dwelling on past mistakes, leaders need to use those experiences to create new and different solutions.

GET A GRIP—LET GO!

- Once you grasp the concept of letting go, you will be well on your way to successfully developing great qualities in yourself and others.

CHANGE FROM THE INSIDE OUT

Acknowledging shortcomings, facing failure, and gaining insight from each failure are necessary steps to personal growth. But to achieve personal and professional success, we must also change the behavior that has led to our shortcomings and failures.

- What one thing do you need to let go of today?
- Which of the negative attitudes listed in this chapter should you pay particular attention to? Which of your habits hampers you most in developing other people?
- What steps can you take to begin focusing your attention on growing and developing others?
- For the next few moments, focus on failure. What was your biggest failure? What did you learn from it? How has it shaped you today? Does thinking about it cause you to want to try again, to relaunch? Or does it make you want to control risk and not try?
- Are there people in your life whom you have blamed for failing you? What steps do you need to take to forgive them?
- Free yourself of any thoughts of failing, and identify one new idea you could try tomorrow.

Thick-and-Thin Togetherness

O n cable television, almost twenty-four hours a day it seems, you can catch sight of a sheriff and his deputy demonstrating core principles of how to develop another person. Yes, Sheriff Andy and his deputy Barney on *The Andy Griffith Show* have this mentoring thing going on.

In many episodes Andy tried to patiently teach Barney about work, love, and life. Then, invariably, Barney struck out to tackle the problem at the core of Andy's teaching, and messed up royally. In spite of Barney's bungling, however, Andy always stood by his friend and coworker, exhibiting a bemused yet persistent patience. Andy was always there for Barney. (But we don't think Barney ever reached the place where he was ready to receive more than one bullet for his gun!)

Although developing your own strengths is important, an equally important task in leadership is maximizing the strengths and potential of the members of your team. If you don't do this well, you may experience a measure of success, but you will also end up very tired and frustrated that so little is getting done. There's just too much to do these days. We all need help. Michael Dell is quoted as saying, "One person cannot do anything alone."[1] He is suggesting that the best leaders nurture highly successful management teams built around complementary skills, shared values, and mentoring.

What image comes to mind when you think of the term *mentor?* You might picture two people sitting at a table in a restaurant, the older person, his or her head topped with waves of shimmering, gray hair, waxing eloquent while the younger listener is furiously scribbling notes on a legal pad. Although this scene may warm our hearts, it seems just a bit out of sync with the real world.

We would like to offer an alternative image of mentoring: Picture two people sitting across from each other in an office. Obviously, an important project is under discussion. The interaction is animated, intense, and often humorous. These people obviously know each other well. Speech is direct and honest. Mutual respect is readily apparent. Some coaching is occurring, but the protégé is not restrained in sharing some insights on the performance of the mentor as well. This relationship is built on trust.

With this picture in mind, we like to define mentoring as a long-term, mutually supportive and enhancing relationship rather than as a relationship in which a highly advanced human being tutors another who stands a step or two below him or her on the developmental ladder.

Another way to envision the mentoring process is to compare it to parenting. In corporate settings we frequently witness nonexistent or very poor "parenting" skills. Executives and managers often fail to recognize that even the most highly qualified person may have significant blind spots or personal or professional characteristics that are awry or underdeveloped. Rather than understanding the need to mentor appropriately and taking the time to discipline, train, coach, or partner with their employees, weak leaders simply hire people and turn them loose to do their jobs.

The basic definition of mentoring implies that the leader and the protégé want to build something that will last a long time. It suggests sticking together and being patient as the learner and the mentor navigate the learning process.

A successful mentoring experience does require a significant prerequisite: *a quality person to mentor.* A leader who hopes to succeed in mentoring must first hire great people. Too often, executives devote too little time to the hiring process. No wonder that down the road the mentoring of a poorly qualified employee resembles corrective discipline more than a shared growth experience.

Assuming the right persons are in the right jobs, a leader must then do everything possible to help those people feel appreciated, supported, empowered, and fully equipped to complete their tasks. In addition, a leader needs to help the other person understand that success is not just "making the numbers" (competency) but includes developing character as well.

A good mentoring experience also requires longevity. The leader and the protégé need to stay at it long enough for the relationship to bear mature fruit.

Some years ago I (Wayne) entered a new career that was absolutely foreign to anything I had ever experienced. Two men, Dan and Bruce, came alongside me and not only taught and encouraged me but held me accountable to my goals and vision—they took me under their wings. The men suggested a weekly meeting where we would each share our problems, concerns, personal failures, and successes. Over time the three of us developed a deep bond of friendship and mutual appreciation. Today, after more than fifteen years, we are separated by geography but still use e-mail and the telephone to stay in touch with one another. We know one another's deepest desires and hold one another accountable for personal integrity and morals. I trust these men with my life.

I (Ron) have a similar story from the mentor's point of view: In the late nineties I was talking to the CEO with whom I had been working for about four years. As we were chatting comfortably at the end of a session, he said to me, "Ron, all of the work you do for us around team building, leadership development, and culture improvement is worth every penny you charge us. But your real value for me as a CEO is when we have these little chats, one on one, in these relaxing, comfortable, and trusting moments."

At that moment I began to realize that the aspect of the business I found most enjoyable—talking openly and honestly with the leaders I worked with—was also the aspect they experienced as most valuable. Since that time a sizable percentage of my consulting business comes from personally coaching and mentoring business leaders.

During these moments of honest interaction, leaders are able to talk with me about personal doubts, concerns over the performance of another individual, and innovative ways to tackle new situations. We can do trial run-throughs of an upcoming presentation, a conference call, or a one-on-one meeting with a boss or colleague. Almost anything that is critical to their performance is open to discussion in this relaxed environment. Even personal situations and career decisions are fair game. The mentoring or coaching role is mainly about creating a safe environment to discuss any topic.

One of the hallmarks of a long-term mentoring relationship is the intentional vulnerability that develops between two people. This means they can easily strip away the outside masks and get down to the issues (both personal and business) that need attention. This kind of openness and willingness to share the truth is a quality found in effective leaders. They refuse to let pride get in the way of open communication that will encourage and assist others and advance the cause of the organization.

If these characteristics of a solid mentoring relationship remind you of a good friendship, you are right. Research data and our experience indicate that, more often than not, mentoring relationships grow over time into lasting friendships. Andy and Barney were "buds" for life.

But if a mentoring relationship is to thrive, men in particular must overcome an issue that many of them struggle with: It's hard for men to be vulnerable with one another, especially in the work environment. In his book *The Friendless American Male*, David Smith writes:

> Men find it hard to accept that they need the fellowship of other men. The simple request, "Let's have lunch together" is likely to be followed with the response, "Sure, what's up?" The message is clear: the independent man doesn't need the company of another man. In fact, the image

of the independent man is that he has few if any emotional needs. Therefore, men must manufacture reasons for being together—a business deal must be discussed or a game must be played. Men often use drinking as an excuse to gather together. Rarely do men plan a meeting together simply because they have a need to enjoy each other's company.

Even when men are frequently together their social interaction begins and remains at the superficial level. Just how long can conversations about politics and sports be nourishing to the human spirit? The same male employees can have lunch together for years and years and still limit their conversation to sports, politics, dirty jokes and comments about the sexual attractiveness of selected female workers in their office or plant. They do not know how to fellowship.[2]

Getting beyond such superficiality takes effort, and at least in the early stages of their relationship, a mentor will have to model appropriate vulnerability to build trust with the protégé. Once the walls start coming down, the process will accelerate and the rewards will be great for both partners. Real issues will be addressed so that genuine personal and organizational growth and change may occur.

What about mentoring involving women? Are their needs and challenges different? Research from Bernice R. Sandler, senior scholar at the Women's Research and Education Institute, says that "at least one study has shown that male mentors were more likely to direct their female protegees and therefore to be disappointed if they [the protegees] did not follow their advice. The study found, in contrast, that female mentors were more likely to encourage and affirm their protegees' career choices; they apparently had less emotional investment in having their protegees follow in their footsteps. Also, male mentors may be largely work focused and ignore personal issues that affect those with whom they are working, while women mentors often show interest in both the personal and professional lives of their students."[3]

Our own experience has revealed that most women prefer a coach from outside their company. While they often would not mind having a male coach, the concerns about sexual overtones and misunderstood motives are often too high to make this a comfortable arrangement. Mentoring the opposite sex (either men mentoring women or women mentoring men) presents challenges, and certainly, if any sexual overtones develop, they need to be confronted and the relationship discontinued.

BECOMING A DEVELOPER OF DYNAMIC CHANGE IN OTHERS

Is there a surefire, can't-fail approach to mentoring effectively in an organizational setting? Probably not. But that should not come as a surprise because, after all, we are talking about relationships between people. However, we do have some ideas, principles, and goals that will help illumine your path to a satisfying and successful mentoring experience.

1. Be an encourager. Encouragement is one of the mentor's most powerful tools for leading another person to higher levels of personal growth. The Greek word for *encouragement* means "coming alongside." This means helping another person by being right there, offering whatever assistance is required.

All of us need encouragement—a word from somebody who believes in us, stands by us, and reassures us. Encouragement renews our courage, refreshes our spirits, and rekindles our hope. Encouragement goes beyond appreciation to affirmation; we appreciate *what* a person does, but we affirm *who* a person is. Affirmation does not insist on a particular level of performance, and it is not earned.

Based on our observation, we do offer one caution related to the issue of encouragement: Many leaders themselves appear to have a low need for personal affirmation and approval and therefore have difficulty understanding the need to encourage and affirm others. If this describes you, you will need to train yourself to give what may feel like over-encouragement to others.

2. Be patient. Mentoring requires a good amount of patience from both parties. The endurance factor is quite important when the person with whom a mentor is working reacts with what might be considered a silly response (in words or actions). It takes patience to watch someone grow and develop into a better person. It takes patience to see missteps and not immediately go in and either change the behavior or solve the problem.

Thomas was the CFO of a large organization, and he took a new hire under his wing. Early on, the new hire, a COO of a smaller division of the same organization, made several mistakes. At issue was the larger organization's culture, which was unfamiliar to the new hire. He had come from a small company with an achievement-driven culture and little bureaucracy. The new company was full of bureaucratic hoops, and the new hire continued to stumble through the process. The CFO remained patient and diligent. They learned together and solved many of the issues. One of the methods used by the CFO was laughter. He never made the new hire feel inferior or guilty. He simply reflected on the COO's actions, taking them for what they were and using them to create an open dialogue for training and learning.

3. Be trustworthy. As a mentor you must exhibit integrity. The person you are mentoring will be open and vulnerable only after watching you live a consistently ethical life. Trustworthiness means being reliable, faithful, and unfailing. Trustworthy leaders are honest and transparent, committed, dedicated, and keep promises and confidences. They also have the moral courage to do the right thing and to stand up for what they believe even when it is difficult to do so.

4. Be an opportunist. A good mentor is always searching for mentoring opportunities. The best mentoring happens in "teachable moments." These impromptu opportunities to share insights and experiences require no formal agenda or time schedule, just a willingness on the leader's part to be available and recognize moments when the other person needs help. This should flow naturally and not be contrived or forced. The protégé may not even realize that a "mentoring moment" has occurred.

Here's an example of how this might look:

One day, Pete, one of the firm's best telesales reps, was listening to a newly hired rep working with a client. When the rep finished the call, Pete said, "Hey, Lee, it's a beautiful day outside. Do you want to take a quick break and walk around the block?" Lee quickly got up out of the chair, and they both left the building.

On the walk Pete told Lee what a great job he had done on the previous call. Lee was successfully using most of the sales principles from the company's training and was building exceptional relationships with his clients. Pete went on to say, "Just one thing, Lee. You might want to slow down a little so you make sure the client completely understands your presentation."

Lee thanked him for the help and eagerly went back to work. Pete, the best on the team, had just told a fellow team member he was doing well. He had also shared a valuable tip to help Lee's sales and performance improve. In just a few moments Pete had encouraged, motivated, and trained the new rep! Pete did not need to wait for a formal training session to mentor Lee. He took Lee aside immediately after overhearing a couple of mistakes. He chose a mentoring moment and tremendously helped a coworker achieve a new level of job performance and customer satisfaction.

The opportunity to mentor exists in every setting where people need to draw on one another's talents to accomplish a goal.

Frank Darabont, director of *The Green Mile*, reflected on Tom Hanks's selfless commitment to helping rising actor Michael Duncan achieve his best:

Fifteen, twenty years from now, what will I remember [about filming *The Green Mile*]? There was one thing—and I'll never forget this: When [Tom] Hanks was playing a scene with Michael Duncan...

As we're shooting, [the camera] is on Michael first, and I'm realizing that I'm getting distracted by Hanks. Hanks is delivering an Academy Award–winning performance, *off-camera*, for Michael Duncan—to give him every possible thing he needs or can use to deliver the best possible performance.

He wanted Michael to do *so* well. He wanted him to look *so* good. I'll never forget that.[4]

In 1999, Michael Clarke Duncan was nominated for an Academy Award in the Best Actor in a Supporting Role category. Tom Hanks, however, was not nominated.

STARTING THE PROCESS

Here, then, are some thoughts on how to begin mentoring others:

First, the best mentoring plans focus primarily on character development and then on skills. As Jim Collins reports, "The good-to-great companies placed greater weight on character attributes than on specific educational background, practical skills, specialized knowledge, or work experience."[5]

Second, we see many mentoring attempts fail because the participants do not sit down together to discuss and set boundaries and expectations. The process flows much better if the participants take time to understand each other's goals, needs, and approaches than if they take a laid-back, let's-get-together approach.

Any mentoring relationship should start with a firm foundation of mutual understanding about goals and expectations. A mentoring plan should be constructed by both individuals, even if it calls for spontaneity in the approach. Nothing is more powerful than motive and heart. Both of the people involved need to fully understand what is driving each of them to want this deeper experience of growth and commitment.

We are currently working with an organization where a senior executive is trying to help a new manager. Incredible as it may seem, the manager was frequently not showing up on time—or at all—for scheduled mentoring appointments. We doubt that he fully understood the senior executive's passion for his personal growth. When they later met to discuss the problem, the senior executive explained why he was willing to get up very early in the morning to help mentor the manager. Once the manager had grasped these basic facts, he started taking the sessions more seriously. *Good idea!*

Although we strongly endorse the notion of mentoring spontaneously during "teachable moments"—such as when Barney locked himself in the jail cell—ideally we suggest using a combination of scheduled and unscheduled opportunities to learn and grow together.

NEED A MENTOR YOURSELF?

Research has shown that leaders at all levels need mentoring. Even though you may be mentoring others successfully, you need a mentor too. Everything we've said in this chapter applies to you. Just put yourself in the protégé's shoes.

There are two issues that we want you to be especially cognizant of:

1. *Vulnerability.* You must open yourself up to your mentor by being "woundable," teachable, and receptive to criticism. The essence of vulnerability is a lack of pride. You cannot be proud and vulnerable at the same time. It takes a focus on humility to be vulnerable.

2. *Accountability.* Commit yourself wholeheartedly to your mentor (or protégé) and put some teeth in the relationship by establishing goals and expected behavior. Accountability should include:

   • "Being willing to explain one's actions.
   • Being open, unguarded, and nondefensive about one's motives.
   • Answering for one's life.
   • Supplying the reasons why."[6]

   Like vulnerability, accountability cannot exist alongside pride. Pride must take a backseat to a person's need to know how she or he is doing and to be held accountable by someone who is trusted.

People who are accountable are humble enough to allow people to come close and support them, and, when they drift off course, they welcome the act of restoration without the pride that says, "I don't need anyone."

TEAM MENTORING

Is it possible to have a somewhat formalized mentoring program in an organization or for one person to mentor large numbers of people? It depends.

We are not fans of highly structured corporate mentoring programs. In reality, these large, generic approaches are often too loose and impersonal to give the life-changing attention we advocate. Developing others is work, some of the most challenging work any of us will ever do. Leaders must be ready to stick with it through thick and thin. A solid mentoring culture will not exist with just a "pretty face." Trust takes a huge blow if you promise to mentor people but fail to follow through over the long haul.

So is mentoring even feasible in a flat organization in which a leader may have eleven to fifteen direct-reports? Our advice is to be careful. Your only reasonable hope is to approach the task with a broader focus on "team."

Bo Schembechler, the great former coach of the University of Michigan football team, was once asked on a radio talk show how he was able to sustain a winning program over so many years when such a large percentage of his best players graduated each year. His response was, "X's and O's are fun, but if you want a winning program, you have to get out with your players and build a team."

Coach Schembechler clearly understood the dynamic and need of mentoring and building a team. His entire mentoring efforts were driven to build teamwork and team execution. He probably felt that his assistant coaches could individually mentor certain players under their care. However, as head coach, Bo Schembechler mentored all of the football players on how to be a successful team. He did it by focusing attention away from individual needs to the greater needs, goals, values, and vision of the team. He did not intend to build individuals; he intended to build a unit.

Too often we have worked with leaders who don't feel it's their job to build a team. Their attitude is that they have great people on the team; they are all successful, mature adults and will get along just fine. Wrong. Coach Schembechler understood the value of actually building a team that eventually would win the Big Ten championship. It would be the team that carried on the Michigan values to the next set of incoming freshman. Building a team was the key to sustaining success over a long period of time in spite of constantly changing team members and conditions.

Mentoring is a life-changing part of development. The goal is to coach and guide people through life transitions and structures, focusing on the "being" rather than the "doing."

In many ways, mentoring resembles a parent who lets a child learn how to feed herself. It can be downright messy! Food ends up on the face, in the hair, on the floor, on Mommy and Daddy—and occasionally in the mouth. Milk is spilled so frequently that a whole industry evolved to provide those nearly spill-proof cups! Parents have two choices: Let their child thrash around and learn how to manipulate a spoon, or continue to feed her themselves. But really there is only one good choice—as is true with mentoring. You just can't spoon-feed a child forever. Neither should you artificially prop up a work associate who must learn to handle responsibilities. You need genuine concern, patience, and a great sense of humor, whether you are teaching a child eating skills or mentoring an employee in how to handle customer complaints. But it's worth the effort. People committed to growing together through thick and thin accomplish great things.

THE ESSENTIALS

- Although developing your own strengths is important, an equally important task in leadership is maximizing the strengths and potential of the members of your team.
- True mentoring relationships are built on trust.
- We like to define mentoring as a long-term, mutually supportive and enhancing relationship rather than as a relationship in which a highly advanced human being tutors another who stands a step or two below him or her on the developmental ladder.
- The basic definition of mentoring implies that the leader and the protégé want to build something that will last a long time.
- A leader who hopes to succeed in mentoring others must first hire great people.
- A leader needs to help the other person understand that success is not just "making the numbers" (competency) but includes developing character as well.
- One of the hallmarks of a long-term mentoring relationship is the intentional vulnerability that develops between two people.
- Men in particular must overcome an issue that many of them struggle with: It's hard for men to be vulnerable with one another, especially in the work environment.

Becoming a Developer of Dynamic Change in Others

- *Be an encourager*—Encouragement renews our courage, refreshes our spirits, and rekindles our hope.
- *Be patient*—It takes patience to watch someone grow and develop into a better person.

- *Be trustworthy*—You must exhibit integrity and be worthy of trust.
- *Be an opportunist*—A good mentor is always searching for mentoring opportunities. Don't wait for formal mentoring sessions. Use "teachable moments" to mentor, teach, and encourage.

Starting the Process

- Focus primarily on character development and then on skills.
- Set boundaries and expectations *together.*
- Use a combination of scheduled and unscheduled opportunities to learn and grow together.

Need a Mentor Yourself?

- Be vulnerable and open to being held accountable. Leaders at all levels need mentoring, and you need a mentor too.

Team Mentoring

- Be careful when mentoring teams. Large, generic approaches to mentoring are often too loose and impersonal to give the life-changing attention we advocate. You may find yourself sacrificing trust and one-on-one vulnerability in team mentoring.

CHANGE FROM THE INSIDE OUT

The ultimate message of mentoring is to nurture positive people. We trust in people. We trust in ourselves and focus on helping and teaching. What changes do you need to make to be a great mentor?

- A proverb says, "Wounds from a friend are better than many kisses from an enemy."[7] What does this mean to you?
- Look for opportunities to mentor other people. What could you cut from your day that could free up the time to encourage someone?
- Choose a person whom you could mentor. How can you help him or her?
- Consider the value of becoming accountable. What walls do you need to pull down to become more accountable and open?

"Favored Are the Steadfast"

Commitment without reflection is fanaticism in action.
But reflection without commitment is the paralysis of all action.

—Coach JOHN MCKAY

William Wallace personified commitment.

The movie *Braveheart* tells the story of this hero-leader. He is the warrior-poet who became the liberator of Scotland in the early 1300s. As the film begins we see that Scotland has been under the iron fist of English monarchs for centuries. Wallace is the first to defy the English oppressors and emerges as the leader of an upstart rebellion. Eventually he and his followers stand up to their tyrants in a pivotal battle.

Wallace inspires his "army" as he shouts, "Sons of Scotland, you have come here to fight as free men, and free men you are!"

That battle is won. Later, though, Wallace is captured by the English and, after refusing to support the king, dies a terrible, torturous death. His last word? "FREEDOM!"[1]

As a leader, Wallace understood the need to commit to personal core values, and he was able to inspire others to join him to the death for a noble, transcending vision: the cause of freedom.

This kind of response from others is what's possible for leaders who understand the clarifying and galvanizing strength of commitment.

Climbing Above the Fog

K nowing what you want is very important.

It's surprising how many people, even those in leadership roles in large organizations, do not really know what they want. They are good people with good motives and good ideas. They work hard and get a lot done. But their values are inconsistent; their vision is not clear. They are wandering in fog.

To ultimately realize the power of commitment, you must be sure of where you are going and what attitudes and behavior will ensure that you arrive at your destination with your head held high.

Commitment has its origins in clearly perceived values and vision.

Long ago, when Wayne and I (Ron) were just lads growing up and forming our first understandings of life, we both were mentored by fathers who knew what kind of boys they wanted around the family house. Both men were committed to a simple core value: honesty.

Telling a lie was the worst thing we could do. Such an act brought great disappointment to these men and resulted in our immediate sentencing and punishment. We quickly gained a deep appreciation for the wisdom of telling the truth. Looking back, we recognize that learning the value of honesty so young has served us well ever since. Being truthful has made us better men and better leaders. Such deep commitment to integrity began when our fathers focused our attention on honesty.

What our dads did also reveals how values and vision interrelate. Our fathers had a vision for the kind of offspring they wanted to produce: men of integrity. They knew that honesty would be a key foundation stone in building individuals with that type of character.

In this chapter we intend to clear some haze and explain how a leader can climb above the fog to find that vantage point where the air is clear and the important destinations can be seen and purposefully pursued.

PERSONAL VALUES

Simply stated, our values reflect what we consider *important*. Usually, they have developed over time and reveal who we really are. Values are motivators; they give us reasons for why we do or don't do things.

Values drive behavior. Typically, we chase what we love. Jesus said it well: "Where your treasure is, there your heart will be also."[1]

Too often we get it backward and find our behavior driving our values. We allow our actions to dictate our fundamental values rather than creating a set of values and standing firm in them. In this situation we allow our "want to" to overtake our "ought to." Since these values usually do not match, we give in and are controlled by the short-term "want to" rather than the longer-term "ought to."

For our purposes in this book, values are defined as "uncompromising, undebatable truths." The emphasis on truth is important because values are not always the more positive human attributes. An example of such warped values is the practice of some inner-city gangs who require members to commit a robbery or worse to prove personal courage and loyalty to the group.

Stephen Covey, in his book *The 7 Habits of Highly Effective People*, writes,

The Character Ethic [set of values as used here] is based on the fundamental idea that there are principles [values] that govern human effectiveness—natural laws in the human dimension that are just as real, just as unchanging and unarguably "there" as laws such as gravity are in the physical dimension.[2]

Commitment is not worth much if you have a distorted vision and rotten values. It is crucial, then, for leaders to develop the right core values. Right actions flow out of right values such as integrity, honesty, human dignity, service, excellence, growth, and evenhandedness. This set of values will determine much about the vision that leaders create and how they work with and through people—essentially how they lead and to what they are committed.

Developing and committing to values is only part of the equation. Leaders also need to form a vision. These two ideas—values and vision—are inseparable. Vision flows from our values, and the values we live by form the platform for our vision. A leader's strength of commitment determines how well he or she will stick to either one.

DEVELOPING VISION

It is important for a leader to be committed to a vision. When professors Warren Bennis and Burt Nanus studied the lives of ninety leaders, they found that "attention through vision" was one of their key leadership strategies.[3] Vision is the ability to look beyond today, beyond the obstacles, beyond the majority opinion and gaze across the horizon of time and imagine greater things ahead. It is the ability to see what is not yet reality.

Vision includes foresight as well as insight. It requires a future orientation. Vision is a mental picture of what could be. It also suggests uniqueness, an implication that something special is going to happen. According to Bennis and Nanus,

The leader's job (and we are talking about any leader, at any level, and anywhere in the company) is to paint the big picture, to convey the vision, giving people a clear sense of what the puzzle will look like when everyone has put the pieces—how it will impact each person where they are—in place. A vision is a mental picture of what tomorrow will look like. A vision should impact each person right where they are. It expresses our highest standards and values. It sets us apart and makes us feel special. It spans years of time and keeps us focused on the future. And if it's to be attractive to more than an insignificant few, it must appeal to all of those who have a stake in it.[4]

How do you develop a vision? Writers James Kouzes and Barry Posner suggest the following:

You feel a strong inner sense of dissatisfaction with the way things are in your community, congregation or company and have an equally strong belief that things don't have to be this way. Envisioning the future begins with a vague desire to do something that would challenge yourself and others. As the desire grows in intensity, so does your determination. The strength of this internal energy forces you to clarify what it is that you really want to do. You begin to get a sense of what you want the organization to look like, feel like, and be like when you and others have completed the journey.[5]

When you have vision, it affects your attitude. You are more optimistic. You envision possibilities rather than probabilities.

Vision requires belief. It requires that you refuse to give in to temptation, doubt, or fear. It is a belief that sustains you through the difficult times. Vision requires commitment and endurance. It takes a willingness to be stretched.

Leaders with vision assume anything is possible. Without vision, we can see a difficulty in every opportunity. As we develop vision, we see an opportunity in every difficulty.

Vision asks leaders to hang tough. There is no magic formula that says, "Everything I see in the future will be fine and will fall into place." Vision differentiates us from others; it sets us apart. It helps leaders attract and retain employees who share a common vision.

Vision is a statement of destination. Leaders need to occupy their time with thinking about how things could be and project themselves into that future. Vision is thinking ahead.

PRODUCING THE VISION

Abraham Lincoln united his followers with the vision of preserving the Union and abolishing slavery. Lincoln successfully gathered people to his vision, based on a strong set of personal values, and he accomplished an incredible feat. How was Lincoln able to do this? How is any leader able to set vision into reality? Consider the following suggestions:

1. *Establish a clear direction.* Have you ever taught someone to drive a car? Both of us have been the "driver's ed" teachers in our respective families. We have seen that as teens learn to drive, their first instinct is to watch the road directly in front of the car. This results in constant course correction—the front wheels turn sharply as the car swerves from roadside shoulder to the center divider, back and forth. When you approach a curve, the swerving worsens! But when young motorists learn to look as far down the road as possible while they drive, the car's path straightens out. They are then able to negotiate

corners, obstacles, and other dangers much more smoothly. A distant reference point makes the path straighter.

2. Focus your attention. We often focus on too many methods and alternatives. Building vision means focusing our attention on that vision. Focus is necessary so that lower priorities do not steal time from the central vision. If the vision is deeply planted in your heart and mind, you can proactively, rather than reactively, respond to outside forces and issues.

3. Articulate values. Leaders need to clearly express their inner values. On what values is a vision based? Team members need to know—and leaders need to share—this basic insight. People knew that Abraham Lincoln was a man of integrity, honesty, hard work, and fairness. These basic values supported his vision of a unified country.

4. Enlist others to help with implementation. In his book *Leading Change* John Kotter writes:

No one individual, even a monarch-like CEO, is ever able to develop the right vision, communicate it to large numbers of people, eliminate all the key obstacles, generate short-term wins, lead and manage dozens of change projects, and anchor new approaches deep in the organization's culture. Weak committees are even worse. A strong guiding coalition is always needed—one with the right composition, level of trust, and shared objective. Building such a team is always an essential part of the early stages of any effort to restructure, reengineer, or retool a set of strategies [or, we may add, move a vision to reality].[6]

5. Communicate, communicate, communicate. Leaders who want to create and implement a vision need to start a fire in the belly of the people they lead. They need to use all available forms of communication to get the word out. It is akin to brand management. A company that wants to launch a new brand will use every form of communication available to get people to try the new products. The same is true with implementing a vision. Leaders cannot over-communicate what they see in the future.

6. *Empower followers.* In order to implement a vision, leaders need to encourage clear buy-in from the people. This requires moving beyond communication to collaboration. The goal is to develop a supportive environment and bring along other people with differing talents and abilities. It also means that when the followers truly understand the vision, the leader needs to step aside and let them do the work to "produce" the vision. The leader needs to give them the authority and responsibility to do the work necessary in order to bring his or her vision to fruition.

We witnessed a meeting recently in which the leader brought together a crossfunctional group to brainstorm some marketing campaign ideas for the company. People from different departments assembled and were led through a planned exercise on corporate marketing focus for the following year. The best idea came from a person far removed from the marketing department. She quite innocently blurted out just the right direction and even suggested a great theme for the entire campaign.

If the leaders of this organization had simply called together the "marketing types," they would have missed a tremendous idea. Or if the leader had done the work alone and not opened it up to input from others, he might not have secured the necessary buy-in from the staff to implement the project. Studies show that when people understand the values and are part of the vision and decision-making process, they can better handle conflicting demands of work and higher levels of stress.[7]

The leadership would also have missed the energy these employees gained from simply being included in a "vision" meeting. After the session several employees came to the leadership and thanked them for the opportunity to help. Those leaders have obviously climbed above the fog and know what they are committed to.

THE ESSENTIALS

- Leaders at every level of the organization need to know what they want.
- To ultimately realize the power of commitment, you must be sure of where you are going and what attitudes and behavior will ensure that you arrive at your destination with your head held high.

PERSONAL VALUES

- Our values reflect what we consider important; they give us reasons for why we do or don't do things.
- Too often we get it backward and find our behavior driving our values.
- Values are defined as "uncompromising, undebatable truths."
- Commitment is not worth much if you have a distorted vision and rotten values. It is critical for leaders to develop the right core values such as integrity, honesty, human dignity, service, excellence, growth, and evenhandedness.

DEVELOPING VISION

- Vision is the ability to look beyond today, beyond the obstacles, beyond the majority opinion and imagine greater things ahead.
- Vision includes foresight as well as insight. It is an internal mental picture of what could be.

- Vision requires that you refuse to give in to temptation, doubt, or fear. Vision requires commitment and endurance.
- Leaders with vision assume anything is possible.

PRODUCING THE VISION

- Establish a clear direction.
- Focus your attention.
- Articulate values.
- Enlist others to help with implementation.
- Communicate, communicate, communicate.
- Empower followers.

CHANGE FROM THE INSIDE OUT

Your values are your platform. They continually communicate who you are and how you work and lead. Your vision sets the agenda. Whether you are part of a small department, a large organization, or a global giant, your vision will set the direction and purpose of the enterprise. You will need a strong sense of commitment and trust to set your vision in motion and deliver it.

- What truly inspires you?
- List your personal values. In what ways do they help you see yourself and the things you pursue more clearly?
- What is your vision? What is your business passion?
- Do you have a clear understanding of how you and/or your organization needs to be different in ten years? Explain.

Standing for Something Greater

ommitment involves rising above our own needs and perspectives to grab hold of a greater good. As psychiatrist and author M. Scott Peck reminds us, "People are searching for a deeper meaning in their lives."[1] The leader who understands this and who responsibly presents a great cause to followers will turn a key in many hearts and unlock vast reservoirs of creativity and productivity.

Standing for something greater relates directly to the values and vision of an organization. A leader's stance for something greater not only meets his or her personal desires, but it strongly resonates with peers, direct-reports, and others who have a stake in the organization.

History presents many examples of great men and women who understood the need to lift up allegiance to something great. These people stood their ground and had the controlled strength to remain focused on the ultimate objective.

Susan B. Anthony was such a person.

Born in 1820 in Adams, Massachusetts, Susan grew up in a Quaker family devoted to a variety of social causes. Equipped with a keen mind and a tenacious spirit, Susan was attracted to the battle to improve the status of women who not only could not vote but were also barred from professions such as law or medicine and could not even enroll in college.

While attending her first women's rights conference at Syracuse in 1852, Susan concluded that "the right which woman needed above every other, the one indeed which would secure to her all the others, was the right of suffrage."[2]

Susan B. Anthony had found her "something-greater" cause, a passionate pursuit that would claim most of her attention and energy for the rest of her life. She worked tirelessly to keep the issue of suffrage before the public by speaking, petitioning Congress and state legislatures, and publishing newspapers.

In 1872 she put feet to her convictions by defying the existing laws and casting a vote in the presidential election. What a scene at shortly after 7 A.M. on Election Day when Susan and several other women marched to their polling place. The voting inspectors were not totally surprised by the appearance of these "lawbreakers" in long skirts. Several days earlier Susan and three of her sisters had encountered stiff resistance at a men's barbershop, which was set up temporarily as a voter registration office. The three young men supervising registration initially refused to let Susan and the others register, and a heated argument ensued. After an hour of debate, a frustrated Susan finally got the inspectors to relent when she told them, "If you refuse us our rights as citizens, I will bring charges against you in Criminal Court and I will sue each of you personally for large, exemplary damages!"[3] This threat turned the tide, and the women were grudgingly allowed to register.

On election day Susan was allowed to fill out the paper ballot and cast her vote for presidential candidate U.S. Grant. But that was not the end of the matter. Later Susan was arrested and charged for casting an illegal vote. Hoping to gain more public attention for the suffrage cause, she refused to post bail (her lawyer paid it out of his own pocket).

At her trial the arguments were long and passionate on both sides. After the prosecution and defense were heard, in a surprising turn of events, the judge told the jury it must return a guilty verdict.

Susan and her supporters were outraged and claimed the trial was a farce. The next day at the sentencing, Susan gave a long, stirring statement that the judge tried repeatedly to interrupt. Ultimately the judge fined her one hundred dollars. Susan never paid the fine, nor did the court ever try to collect it.

Later, after reviewing the case, the U.S. Supreme Court decided women still could not vote. Unwilling to abandon her great cause, Susan fought on faithfully until her death in 1906. It wasn't until 1920, with the ratification of the nineteenth amendment to the U.S. Constitution, that women were finally given the right to vote in the United States.[4]

The self-sacrifice of women like Susan B. Anthony and their vision for something greater than themselves led to significant cultural changes in the United States. Today, many take it for granted that women can attend college, work in any chosen profession, and have access to every right available to men. This was not the case in 1872.

People in organizations can be caught in a similar trap. They don't see anything past Friday's paycheck. The organization offers them little vision, few or inconsistent values, and little or no opportunity to achieve the Growth Achievement Path (GAP) we discussed earlier. Granted, not every situation embodies a culture-altering, transcendent cause like woman's suffrage. But trusted leaders know how important a higher goal is for individual and organizational well-being. They always point the way to something greater.

Leading a Team to a Great Cause

Just having personal commitment to a great cause is not enough for a leader. The vision for "something beyond" must be successfully transferred to the entire group, whether it be a small staff, a department, an entire organization, a state, or a nation.

People do not like to be put in boxes, and just as important, people do not like to be in the dark, outside the door where company values and vision are shaped. People are less energized and tend to drift when they are unsure of how they should be operating within an organization. People need to see their leaders' commitment to values, and they want a part in helping to shape their organization's core values and vision.

Many companies start with the right motivation. They talk about their values and they create high aspirations, but these same companies don't really live by them.

The Australian Institute of Management and Hong Kong Management Association found that when leaders worked hard to develop consensus around shared values people were more positive. They also discovered that leaders who engage in dialogue around common values develop a stronger sense of personal effectiveness in their people than leaders who do not.[5]

Leaders who form corporate values, vision, and strategy in a vacuum or just in the executive suite lack the humility and commitment to move beyond themselves and include others who have solid ideas and opinions on what should define the company's values. When leaders don't talk about the company's values and vision, people feel alienated and less energized.

John Kotter and James Heskett found that firms with a strong corporate culture and a foundation of shared values (values developed together with employees) significantly outperformed other firms in revenue, stock value, and profits.[6] Who wouldn't want those results?

When working to plant a vision and sense of a greater cause in a team, you must first ensure that values are understood and owned. This is accomplished initially by cataloging the personal values of individual team members. When the personal values of individuals are understood, team values begin to emerge.

The following story illustrates the steps that one dynamic business leader took to win support for a great cause in his organization.

After agreeing with his executive team on a set of core values, the CEO of this large firm got so interested in employee input on team values that he asked a consulting team to go to six different locations and determine the values of the two hundred to three hundred employees at each site. In team settings, it is often easy to agree on the first five to seven values; however, discussions get very interesting as teams round out the full list of values that will govern their individual behavior and business practices. Using an audience response system, the consultants asked each table-grouping of employees to discuss and develop team values. Next, they worked on "room" values.

Upon completion of the six-city tour, the employee list of values was compared to the executive list. The two lists were surprisingly similar. After some final discussions and some tweaking of the list by the company's leaders, a final list of values was issued.

Although the operative values came down from on high, every employee who had participated had a personal stake in and loyalty to the list. The company-wide discussion had galvanized the organization not just to a set of core values but to a gigantic something-greater goal pursued by the company's CEO. This company desperately needed to reverse a quarter-century of declining market share for its products. The CEO used this exercise in determining values as well as a great amount of day-to-day, hands-on involvement with key personnel to successfully "sell" his organization on the dream of a huge reversal of the company's fortunes. The entire company bought into the dream and now shared his passion for something greater.

STEPS TO STANDING FOR SOMETHING GREATER

As a leader, how do you get from here to there if a vision for something greater currently does not exist within your organization? Consider the following ideas.

1. Clean up your act. It is difficult to convince others to stand for something greater if your own life and values are mediocre. Make no mistake: Regardless of what you hear from assorted voices, your personal moral standards are inseparably linked to long-term leadership success.

We worked with a vice president of a large company who appeared very successful but did not adhere to high personal standards. He was very good at what he did and had a magnificent reputation. He had also successfully navigated through some tough spots for the company.

This V.P. liked to call himself "a player." Essentially, being a player meant that he messed around outside of marriage. He did not see this as wrong (pride talking) and told us it would not affect his people or the quality of the job they were doing (pride again). In his arrogance he thought he could keep his two worlds—work and extramarital cheating—separate.

Twenty-four months later, the vice president's inability to control his pride and lust cost him everything, including his job. His clever scheme fell apart. His self-focus swallowed him up.

It's fun to be a leader, flattering to have influence, and invigorating to have a room full of people cheering your every word. It is a powerful boost to set a direction for the troops and then draw them out to march toward the goal. However, nothing will spoil this pretty picture more quickly than a willful, proud attitude.

Author and speaker Joyce Meyer writes,

> How can you tell you have a problem with pride? Examine yourself. If you have an opinion about everything, you have a problem with pride. If you are judgmental, you have a problem with pride. If you can't stand to be corrected, you have a problem with pride. If you rebel against authority, if you want to take all the credit and glory to yourself, if you say "I" too often, then you have a problem with pride.[7]

Pride can cause an uncontrolled will, which is fatal in a leader's life.

2. Examine your values. While attending seminary, Martin Luther King Jr. read extensively in the areas of history, philosophy, and religion. With each book and each discipline, he questioned what he truly believed. As he read, learned, and reflected, he molded his values and vision on the anvil of discovery.

This kind of personal searching is essential for every good leader. How can you clarify values, set vision, get beyond yourself, and stand for something greater if you have not participated in the intense, personal struggle to clarify, define, and establish who you are as a person? As a leader you will be asked many questions—economic, moral, and personal. How will you know what answers to give unless you have wrestled with some of the questions? How can you shape who you are without struggling with opposing values?

The result of this struggle is personal integrity and credibility. Abraham Lincoln did not just "discover" his vision for America. As a young man, he saw the ravages of poverty and exclusion. As a lawyer, he defended the rights of people. As a father, he witnessed the death of two of his children. Lincoln struggled and fought with others as well as himself, and the result was a clearer picture of his personal values and a more defined vision. The result was also a president of high integrity and purpose.

3. Elevate people to a higher purpose. Lincoln motivated people by leaving his office and spending time with everyone in the government and military hierarchy. One hundred and twenty years later, Tom Peters dubbed this kind of management style as "management by walking around." When a leader gets out and interacts with all the people, the vision is communicated, the values are acted upon, the leader is observed, and the people are inspired.

Whether or not leaders literally walk around, the important factor is elevating and transforming people to serve a higher purpose. People respond by seeking higher moral standards for themselves and the organization. A higher purpose serves to develop common ground, and the common ground leads to energy in attaining goals. It creates a center of importance around which the team can rally and be unified.

4. Seize the higher ground. "John Gardner, Stanford professor, former secretary of Health, Education, and Welfare and founding chairperson of Common Cause, has written that there are four moral goals of leadership:

1. Releasing human potential
2. Balancing the needs of the individual and the community
3. Defending the fundamental values of the community
4. Instilling in individuals a sense of initiative and responsibility"[8]

Gardner notes that concentrating on these aspects will direct you to higher purposes. They take the focus off of you and place it on the people around you. They enable you to let go of the things in life that do not matter and instead make time and create energy for the things that do matter: the welfare of others, the organization, and the larger community.

5. Recognize the cost. Standing for something greater often exacts a significant price. Senator John McCain, speaking at the 1988 Republican National Convention, told the story about a special soldier whom he met while a prisoner of war in Vietnam.

McCain spent over five years imprisoned by the North Vietnamese in what was called the "Hanoi Hilton." In the first few years of his imprisonment, McCain and the other soldiers were kept in isolation. Then in 1971 the North Vietnamese put the prisoners in more open quarters with up to forty men in a room.

One of the men in Senator McCain's cell was Mike Christian. Mike was from the rural south and had joined the navy when he was seventeen. Eventually he had become a pilot and, after being shot down in 1967, was captured and imprisoned.

As the prison rules eased, the men were allowed to receive packages from home. McCain stated, "In some of these packages were handkerchiefs, scarves and other items of clothing."[9] The prisoners' uniforms were basic blue, and Mike Christian took some white and red cloth from the gifts and fashioned an American flag inside his shirt.

Mike's shirt became a symbol for the imprisoned Americans. Every day, after lunch, they would put Mike's shirt on the wall and recite the Pledge of Allegiance. You can imagine that, for these men, this was an emotional and significant daily event.

One day the Vietnamese found Mike Christian's homemade flag. They destroyed it and later that evening, as an example to the other prisoners, beat Mike for over two hours.

McCain remembers, "I went to lie down to go to sleep. As I did, I happened to look in the corner of the room. Sitting there beneath that dim light bulb, with a piece of white cloth a piece of red cloth, and another shirt and bamboo needle was my friend, Mike Christian. Sitting there with his eyes almost shut from beating, making another American flag."[10]

Lt. Commander Mike Christian is a real-life example of how leaders can shift their focus away from themselves, their power, and their potential to something (or someone) outside themselves, seeking the greater good for others as well as for the organization and the community at large.

Standing for something greater moves leaders past their own interests to something that benefits everyone. It takes controlled strength not to fall back to the shortsightedness of doing things only for selfish gain or selfish reasons.

In a POW camp Mike Christian was willing to stand for a symbol of the country he loved. His actions inspired others to stand strong as well and not to surrender hope. That's the power of commitment to something greater.

THE ESSENTIALS

- Commitment involves rising above our own needs and perspectives to grab hold of a greater good.

- A leader's stance for something greater not only meets his or her personal desires, but it strongly resonates with peers, direct-reports, and others who have a stake in the organization.
- Trusted leaders will point the way to something greater so that people within their organizations can see past Friday's paycheck.

Leading a Team to a Great Cause

- People are less energized and tend to drift when they are unsure of how they should be operating within an organization. People need to see their leaders' commitment to values, and they want a part in helping to shape their organization's core values and vision.
- When leaders don't talk about the company's values and vision, people feel alienated and less energized.
- Leaders must first ensure that values are understood and owned by the team.

Steps to Standing for Something Greater

- *Clean up your act*—Your personal moral standards are inseparably linked to long-term leadership success.
- *Examine your values*—The intense, personal struggle to clarify, define, and establish who you are as a person is essential for every good leader.
- *Elevate people to a higher purpose*—People respond by seeking higher moral standards for themselves and the organization. A higher purpose serves to develop common ground.
- *Seize the higher ground*—Take the focus off yourself and place it on the people around you. Make time and create energy for the things that matter.
- *Recognize the cost*—Standing for something greater often exacts a significant price. Leaders must shift their focus away from themselves, their power,

and their potential to something (or someone) outside themselves, seeking the greater good for others as well as for the organization and the community at large.

CHANGE FROM THE INSIDE OUT

Standing for something greater means standing for something other than yourself. The cause is not "all for you"; it is something greater of which you are part. You bring value, but so do others. People whose view doesn't reach outside themselves are ultimately limited to their own box of knowledge and vision.

- Why do you go to work? What is driving you? Is it self-gratification or doing something for the greater good?
- Do other people know what drives you?
- Take time to re-evaluate the following: What you are standing for? What do you believe in? What drives you?

"Favored Are Those Desperate for Excellence"

*He reduced complexities to essentials, making the game easier
to learn. He wanted simple things done with consistent
excellence rather than complicated things done poorly.*

—Journalist WILLIAM FURLONG on Vince Lombardi

The game of golf requires proper equipment, good skills, countless hours of practice, tons of patience, and luck. But maybe more than any of these, golf requires a highly refined ability to concentrate. Another word for this is *focus.*

Watch Tiger Woods as he completes another double-digit win on the PGA tour: His expression before every shot is somber. His eyes are on his business. He normally talks only to his caddy—and himself. Tiger is focused. Only after the ball plunks into the cup at the eighteenth hole and the scorecard is calculated and signed will you see much of that famous Tiger smile. Then he'll talk to reporters and others.

Tiger's demeanor on the golf course is shared by most professional golfers. That's why Chi Chi Rodriguez, a golfer on tour some years ago, was so wildly popular with fans. During one Bob Hope Desert Classic, the easygoing Chi Chi (who tackled difficult putts with a toreador's look in his eye, drawing his putter like a sword from an invisible scabbard) was in rare form. Every ball flew from his club face with tremendous power and accuracy. He tore up the course, having a birdie chance on nearly every hole. Chi Chi was confident, in control of his game, and having fun.

Having fun? Yes. On this day, like most days for Rodriguez, he was having fun. He talked nonstop to the crowd, joking and wisecracking his way down each fairway, until he reached his golf ball. Then, for a few minutes, he was all business. He practiced his swing. He measured the distance to the green. He practiced again. Then he got into his stance, riveted his eyes on the ball, and "whap!" he hit the ball straight down the fairway or near the pin.

After he noted the path of his shot, back he went to talking and performing for the crowd.

Chi Chi Rodriguez is an example of a focused person: one minute a jokester, the next a serious professional golfer, ready to fire off a sensational shot. Although he could make the crowd roar with enjoyment, when it was time to hit the ball, Chi Chi focused himself, reviewed his goal and objective, and pursued his desired result. Nothing could distract him.

Leaders need that kind of focus. Jesus once said to his team that no one "can serve two masters."[1] That's a reality in all of life and certainly supports the importance of focus for leaders who want to keep themselves and their teams on target.

We have all had days when a variety of organizational "fires" needed our attention. We devoted long hours to doing "good" and often important tasks. But as darkness fell and we headed for home, we knew we had not done the most important thing. That's what happens without focus.

As we will explore in this section, focus and passion are like blood brothers in achieving goals. Pardon what may be a bad pun, but we urge you to *focus* carefully on what we have to say in the following chapters! Are you ready to learn how to focus on the ball in your own game as Chi Chi Rodriguez and Tiger Woods do in theirs?

Doing the Right Things Right

The sun is a powerful source of light as well as energy. Every hour of every day the sun showers the earth with millions, if not billions, of kilowatts of energy. We can, however, actually tame the sun's power. With sunglasses and sunscreen, the sun's power is diffused, and we can be out in it with little or no negative effects.

A laser, by contrast, is a weak source of light and energy. A laser takes a few watts of energy and focuses them into a stream of light. This light, however, can cut through steel or perform microsurgery on our eyes. A laser light is a powerful tool when it is correctly focused.

Leaders cease to be powerful tools when they are out of focus and their energy is dispersed rather than targeted. The following is a not-uncommon scenario:

You know the drill. It's Monday morning. You arrive at work exhausted from a weekend spent entertaining the kids, paying bills, and running errands. You flick on your PC—and 70 new emails greet you. Your phone's voice-mail light is already blinking, and before you can make it stop, another call comes in. With each ring, with each colleague who drops by your office uninvited, comes a new demand—for attention, for a reaction, for a decision, for your time. By noon, when you take 10 minutes to gulp down a sandwich at your desk, you already feel over-worked, overcommitted—overwhelmed.[1]

Rather than resembling a laser, too often we seem like the sun, just going up and down, splashing our energy anywhere and everywhere.

David Allen, one of the world's most influential thinkers on personal pro-ductivity, argues that the challenge is not managing our time, but managing our focus. He believes that with all that is being thrown at leaders, they lose their ability to respond. However, he is quick to add that most leaders create the speed of it all because we allow all that stuff to enter into our lives.

What happens to our energy? Allen says,

If you allow too much dross to accumulate in your "10 acres"—in other words, if you allow too many things that represent undecided, untracked, unmanaged agreements with yourself and with others to gather in your personal space—that will start to weigh on you. It will dull your effectiveness.[2]

Not only will your effectiveness be dulled but so will your power. Instead of being like a steel-cutting laser, you will be like the sun, putting out energy with no focus. There needs to be focus because life is not just about running faster or putting out more energy.

Another problem with unfocused energy is stress. When leaders are so wrapped up in all that is going on around them, they lose their ability to respond effectively. The stress comes from not performing at the level of expectation, which causes more stress. Leaders need to find ways to pull away or systematize the "stuff" so they can focus on leveraging their passion and realizing their goals.

Daniel Phillips, chairman and chief executive officer of SilverBack Tech-nologies, says,

I've been innovating, building and growing start-ups for more than 15 years. I am energized by working with emerging technologies and have years of experience leading companies through the important growth phases from start-up to public offering or private placement, and beyond. Having led several ventures through these challenging phases, I have learned that the most important leadership quality is "focus."[3]

With so much going on around leaders, focus may seem impossible or improbable to achieve. Employees, phones, pagers, e-mail, cell phones, problems, crises, home, family, boards of directors, and other people or things demand so much. We tend to spend our time managing the tyranny of the urgent rather than concentrating our efforts on the relevant and important things that make or break an organization.

So what should we do? Is it possible to better focus your focus?

We have found that two personal qualities combine optimally to create a leader of highly developed focus: passion and achievement. These form the boundaries of focus.

PASSIONATELY-FOCUSED LEADERS

Staying focused is virtually impossible without passion. So how do you identify and capitalize on your passion in the leadership setting?

Passion is a craving deep within us, that yearning for something we feel we just must have. It surfaces in a multitude of ways. For example, consider the story of Patrick (Pádraic) Henry Pearse.

Headmaster at St. Edna's, a small private college south of Dublin, Pearse's passion was Ireland's heritage, something he feared was being destroyed by the domination of the English.

Pearse was by nature a gentle man who could never harm even the smallest creature. He had spent his life helping his students understand and pursue their own big dreams. Pearse certainly was not considered a militant or a revolutionary. Yet he was driven by his passion for Ireland.

No longer able to watch the nation's language, culture, and history eroding, he felt it was time "to pursue his own great goals that, in his words, 'were dreamed in the heart and that only the heart could hold.'"[4]

He embraced the cause to reclaim Ireland and within a year was a leader of the Easter Rising, the Irish rebellion of 1916. After days of intense fighting, the British army defeated the revolutionaries, and on May 3, 1916, Pearse and others were executed in a jail in Dublin. The British leaders mistakenly thought this would put an end to the rebellion. But they did not understand the power of a person's passion, as people across Ireland embraced Pearse's ideas for saving Ireland and dreaming big dreams.

In 1921, Ireland declared freedom from England, and Pearse's passion and dreams for the Irish culture came to fruition. Pádraic Henry Pearse's passion ultimately forced a nation to find itself.[5]

Finding our passion includes dreaming big. Ask yourself some questions:

- What is my burning passion?
- What work do I find absorbing, involving, engrossing?
- What mission in life absolutely absorbs me?
- What is my distinctive skill?

Answers to questions like these will point you to your passion.

A friend of ours, the late Leonard Shatzkin, had a passion for mathematics that helped him become a pioneer in understanding the technicalities of inventory management. He developed a model of inventory control using linear regression that proved to be revolutionary for two companies he headed. But his passion didn't just stop with benefits for his own organizations. Leonard then devoted the rest of his professional career to telling anyone who would listen about maximizing return on investment and minimizing overstocks.

That's what passion is like; one way or another it demands expression.

Even after his death, the effects of Leonard's passion live on. His ideas and systems serve many individuals and organizations well.

Too often we allow old habits, the rigors of everyday life, and our ongoing fears or frustrations to impede our passion. We are cautioned by friends: "Don't be so idealistic." "Don't be so daring." "What if you fail?" These kinds of comments can shrink our passion so that we settle for working in fields away from our passion. We abandon it, we make do, and we play it safe.

Just as a mighty river needs a channel, passion needs a channel and a goal. Without such restraint, the result is a flood, a natural disaster. You need to make certain that you control your passion, not the other way around.

Sir Walter Scott once noted, "He who indulges his sense in any excess renders himself obnoxious to his own reason; and to gratify the brute in him, displeases the man and sets his two natures at variance."

Properly focused passion changes us for the better and often helps shape organizations or, in the case of Pádraic Pearse, even nations. So dream big. Identify what motivates you to get up in the morning. Discover where you can make a difference, based on what "floats your boat." Some people spend their lives looking at the flyspecks on the windshield of life. Dreaming big and fulfilling your passion help you look past the flyspecks to the beautiful world on your horizon.

ACHIEVEMENT-MOTIVATED LEADERS

Along with passion, a desire to achieve motivates a leader to a higher level of focus.

We have concluded that leaders with an achievement-motivated style (balanced by humility) have the most constructive approach to work. Typically, they do not waste time on projects or matters outside their vision. They determine what is important, that "something great," and they seek to achieve it.

For more than twenty years, David C. McClelland and his associates at Harvard University studied people who had the urge to achieve.

McClelland's research led him to believe that the need for achievement is a distinct human motive that can be distinguished from other needs. [His experiment involved asking participants] to throw rings over a peg from any distance they chose. Most people tended to throw at random—now close, now far away; but individuals with a high need for achievement seemed carefully to measure where they were most likely to get a sense of mastery—not too close to make the task ridiculously easy or too far away to make it impossible. They set moderately difficult but potentially achievable goals. [We've determined, based on our experience, that achievable goals are those with a 70 to 80 percent likelihood of success.]

McClelland maintains [that]…achievement-motivated people are not gamblers. They prefer to work on a problem rather than leave the outcome to chance.… Achievement-motivated people take the middle ground, preferring a moderate degree of risk because they feel their efforts and abilities will probably influence the outcome. In business, this aggressive realism is the mark of the successful entrepreneur.…

Another characteristic of achievement-motivated people is that they seem to be more concerned with personal achievement than with the rewards of success. They do not reject rewards, but the rewards are not as essential as the accomplishment itself. They get a bigger "kick" out of winning or solving a difficult problem than they get from any money or praise they receive.[6]

Ralph Waldo Emerson said, "The reward of a thing well done is to have done it." Every January millions of people watch the Super Bowl. During the awards ceremony after the game, we see players with big smiles. What are they shouting about? Not about money or fame, but about the ring. Each player on the winning team gets a championship ring—a symbol of reaching the pinnacle of the sport. Nothing else compares to having that ring. It is proof of the ultimate achievement in football. That's what motivates an achievement-oriented person.

Lastly, achievement-motivated people need feedback. They seek situations in which they get concrete feedback that they define as job-relevant. In other words, they want to know the score.

People with a high need for achievement get ahead because, as individuals, they are producers. They get things done.

Sometimes, however, when they are promoted, when their success depends not only on their own work but on the activities of others, they may become less effective. Since they are highly job-oriented and work to their capacity, they tend to expect others to do the same. As a result, they may lack the interpersonal skills (we refer to this as the encouragement or humility leadership style) and patience necessary for being effective managers of people who are not as achievement-motivated.

FOCUS IS AS DIFFICULT AS HITTING A BASEBALL

The importance of focus cannot be overestimated. And channeling your passion into meaningful achievement is one of the toughest things you can do.

Pete Rose, the baseball player with the most hits of anyone who ever played the game, once said, "See the ball, hit the ball." Sure, Pete!

Think of the challenge: A pitcher stands sixty feet, six inches away from you with the goal of throwing a round object, three inches (seven centimeters) in diameter, past you. In your hands is a round, tapered pole, thirty-two to thirty-six inches in length, otherwise known as a bat. Your goal is to swing the pole and hit the ball only when it enters a small predefined area called the strike zone. (Note: You are referred to as a batter until you actually hit the ball!) In the hand of a professional pitcher, the round object will arrive to meet your bat traveling ninety-plus miles per hour. No wonder even the best batters generally only become hitters in about one-third of their attempts. That's not a success ratio for which we would compliment a brain surgeon or a litigation attorney.

I (Wayne) once attended a reception at the Louisville Slugger Museum where the world-famous bats are crafted. Amid the memorabilia of the museum is a caged area where you can select a pitcher (folks like Roger Clemens or Randy Johnson) who then appears on video on the big-screen monitor and throws a pitch to a stuffed catcher. The radar gun shows the ball (coming from a hole in the video monitor) approaching at ninety miles per hour.

While I was watching this impressive display, former major league pitcher Orel Hershiser came up and overheard me say—as the ball whizzed by—"I could hit that." To which Mr. Hershiser instantly chuckled and commented, "No, you couldn't!"

He was right, of course. To hit a baseball requires great skill, a lot of practice, and our favorite word of the moment: *focus*. Pete Rose remains the all-time master of focus in baseball. It is reported that he could actually pick up the spin of the ball as it left the pitcher's hand. Therefore he could "read" how the baseball seams were tumbling or curving and detect the kind of pitch that was coming at his bat. Good eyesight? Perhaps. Great focus? Absolutely. Rose was so intent on getting a hit that nothing robbed him of focus.

Achieving such consistent focus is a quality of every effective leader. In his book *In Search of Excellence*, Tom Peters called focus "sticking to the knitting," which means that successful companies do not stray far from their central skill. Leaders of excellent organizations keep everyone's eyes focused on "the ball" by not allowing distractions to drift them away from the core of what they do best.

That's what we like to call "doing the right things right."

THE ESSENTIALS

- Leaders cease to be powerful tools when they are out of focus and their energy is dispersed rather than targeted.
- When leaders are so wrapped up in all that is going on around them, they lose their ability to respond effectively.
- We tend to spend our time managing the tyranny of the urgent rather than concentrating our efforts on the relevant and important things that make or break an organization.

Passionately-Focused Leaders

- Passion is a craving deep within us, that yearning for something we feel we just must have.
- Too often we allow old habits, the rigors of everyday life, and our ongoing fears or frustrations to impede our passion.
- Dreaming big and fulfilling your passion help you look past the flyspecks to the beautiful world on your horizon.

Achievement-Motivated Leaders

- Leaders with an achievement-motivated style (balanced by humility) have the most constructive approach to work.
- "Aggressive realism is the mark of the successful entrepreneur."
- "Achievement-motivated people seem to be more concerned with personal achievement than with the rewards of success."
- Achievement-motivated people need feedback.
- Achievement-motivated people get things done.

Focus Is as Difficult as Hitting a Baseball

- Channeling your passion into meaningful achievement is one of the toughest things a leader can do.
- Leaders of excellent organizations keep everyone's eyes focused on "the ball" by not allowing distractions to drift them away from the core of what they do best.

CHANGE FROM THE INSIDE OUT

My (Wayne's) home in Michigan had a nice, flower-filled backyard that attracted rabbits. My dog just loved chasing the rabbits but never succeeded in catching one. She was certainly fast enough; that was not the problem. Her predicament was that she could not decide which rabbit to chase. The lesson: If you chase two (or more) rabbits, they all will escape.

- High-achievement people do the hardest things first; low-achievement people do the easiest. Do you focus on the easy rather than the important but difficult? Explain.
- Sometimes people lose focus because they are trying to please too many people. What drives your behavior: a need for approval or a focused purpose?
- Are you only focused on what your boss tells you to do, or is there a greater purpose to your work?
- How many rabbits are you trying to chase today?

Keeping the Band in Tune

t's all well and good to be a focused leader. That's essential for helping an entire organization lock in and stay on target. But the supreme returns are reserved for focused teams. Just as every leader needs to clarify issues concerning personal passion and achievement, the team must undergo a similar process.

Ron Rex, field vice president of Allstate Insurance, says:

On any given Monday, American business opens up their doors with no clue as to what or when to focus. A leader creates extreme focus!... In order to create extreme focus a leader must develop a constant flow of information that describes the progress toward a goal. On any given day, the culture of an organization will create distractions to goals. These distractions can be the normal business flow of others to out and out combat against current achievement. A leader that intends to create extreme focus on a goal or set of goals must be prepared to fend off organizational disruption from those led. This is achieved by creating an atmosphere of work and information that at times may seem attacking to the status quo but must always lure the team to focus harder on fewer things. In American business today, focus is the one weapon that is not subject to the decisions of others.[1]

While consulting with one of our client organizations on leadership matters, we kept hearing from the high-level executive team that they were all averaging more than eighty hours a week. During the training we did with this group, the topic of the heavy work schedule kept surfacing.

We decided to put what we were doing on pause and take a closer look. Some questions needed answering: First, how could these executives keep up this schedule without destroying themselves, their families, and their teams? Second, with such demands on their time, how would they be able to change ingrained habits and actually start doing this "leadership thing" that they knew was important, but they never seemed able to focus on long enough to accomplish? Would our recommendations, if followed, now cause them to have to work ninety hours per week?

To get hard data on how these executives were allocating their time resources, we decided to use the Stephen Covey view of time management found in his book *The 7 Habits of Highly Effective People.* Covey's Time Management Matrix[2] shows four categories of activities:

We asked the team to spend two weeks tracking their time and scrupulously recording what they were doing during these 80-hour marathons. We tallied the results and created a page on a flip chart for each person, cataloging that 8 of their 80 hours went to task A, 6 hours went to task B, and so on. All 160 hours were accounted for in this way.

The group assembled to hear the results. We wish we had a videotape of the assorted jaw-dropping responses we observed as we first revealed individual patterns and then moved on through a discussion process for the entire group. It was interesting and a bit entertaining when one person would identify an item as Quadrant III (urgent, but not important) and someone else would say, "Time out! If you don't do that task for me, I can't get my work done (Quad-

	Urgent	Not Urgent
Important	**I** ACTIVITIES: Crises Pressing problems Deadline-driven projects	**II** ACTIVITIES: Prevention, PC activities Relationship building Recognizing new opportunities Planning, recreation
Not Important	**III** ACTIVITIES: Interruptions, some calls Some mail, some reports Some meetings Proximate, pressing matters Popular activities	**IV** ACTIVITIES: Trivia, busy work Some mail Some phone calls Time wasters Pleasant activities

rant I)!" It took a great deal of negotiation to reach a team consensus on which activities belonged in which quadrants. However, through those negotiations, we discovered just exactly what each person needed.

In many cases one person or team was generating an entire report that took a great deal of time, while the person who needed the data might use only a single crucial piece of data from the entire report. Once we determined that the one piece of data could be generated easily and, in many cases, could be retrieved on demand by the recipient from a database, a gigantic amount of busywork was eliminated.

After completing the negotiations over quadrant assignments, we added up all the hours and determined that about 20 percent of the hours fell in Quadrants I and II (the categories that really matter if you want to focus the team), while 80 percent fell in the less important Quadrant III.

You can imagine the stunned silence that settled like a black cloud in the room. Finally one executive said, "You mean we accomplished all of our important work in sixteen hours and the other sixty-four hours each week were spent on busywork?" The answer was yes. More silence followed.

How had this bright, talented, and obviously hard working "band" gotten so out of tune, so unbalanced? For one thing, they had never sat down together for this kind of discussion and negotiation. The positive result was that they eliminated a tremendous amount of busywork right on the spot. As a team, they came to grips with the focus-destroying enemy called "the tyranny of the urgent."

If we stopped by your place of business and did the same exercise, what might the results be? Have you and your team identified the *important* versus the *urgent?* Do you spend your time and energy on the *important?*

Al Ries writes,

> In my experience, nobody wants to focus unless forced to do so. I've worked on many different problems over the years at companies large and small, and I find one consistent theme: every company tends to go from order to disorder.[3]

Don't let that happen in your organization. Work hard at focusing the team.

BALANCING INNOVATION AND EXECUTION

At some point, every leader seems to grapple with the balance between innovation and execution. Many leaders struggle with the notion that one great idea will save the day for the organization. Others spend an inordinate amount of time focusing on "getting out the laundry" and not on new ideas.

We believe that innovation for innovations' sake can be detrimental. Innovation is best when it helps get things done. A clear vision and strategy are not enough. Competitors have this as well. Success comes from effectively *executing* strategies and objectives as well as anticipating and preparing for future contingencies. Successful organizations accomplish their objectives faster than their competitors.

Innovation results from creative ideas successfully implemented. Execution and strategy result in competitive advantage.

It seems that everyone wants to innovate, but in practical, day-to-day leadership, only what is accomplished matters. A significant part of getting things done is focus.

We used to work with the leadership of an international organization. The founder was a man of tremendous vision and creativity. It seemed he had new, out-of-the-box ideas every day. Fortunately for him and the organization, his senior leadership team consisted of people who understood focus and execution. They had the ability to take his ideas and, in most cases, make them work.

One idea, however, was a complete flop. The organization lost millions of dollars. Why? Because the idea was well out of the organization's scope. It lacked focus, was not part of the organization's passion, and failed to be executed. The formula for this organization's success required team focus and execution, not just the leader's innovative ideas.

Ram Charan, in his *Fortune* magazine cover story "Why CEOs Fail," points out the primary reason CEOs do not make the grade: "It's bad execution…not getting things done, being indecisive, not delivering on commitments."[4] They have plenty of good ideas and strategies, but in many cases they lack the ability to execute them.

Charan has also written,

People think of execution as the tactical side of business, something leaders delegate while they focus on the perceived "bigger" issues. This idea is completely wrong. Execution is not just tactics—it is a discipline and a system. It has to be built into a company's strategy, its goals, and its culture. And the leader of the organization must be deeply engaged in it.[5]

Innovation is a strong gift. It helps companies find new markets, new products, and new customers. Innovation alone, however, does not matter. Innovation requires focus, and part of that focus is execution or achievement.

THE ACHIEVING TEAM

"I would perform better if…" This is a good opening statement to ask members of your team to complete in order to find out how well everyone is focusing.

Thomas Gilbert, author of *Human Competence,* found that

- Thirty-five percent of people would answer, "[I would perform better if] I knew what the exact expectations of the job were and had more specific job feedback and better access to information."
- Twenty-six percent of workers would respond, "[I would perform better if] I had better tools and resources to work with."
- Fourteen percent said, "[I would perform better if] I had better financial and non-financial incentives for doing my work."[6]

Expectations, feedback, and incentives are key requirements for building an achievement-oriented team. Organizations expend a great amount of time and money on training people to help them become better achievers. They should also channel resources into teaching leaders how to form realistic expectations, provide proper support, and set achievable goals with appropriate incentives. Organizations and their leaders continually try to fix the individual, but if they would just change the environment (information, resources, and incentives), they would see drastic changes and results.

The good news is that these factors are easily developed and integrated into the life of a team. Let's take a look at how to get this done.

Energizing the Team with Vision

As we have indicated earlier, people are hungry to be led and will gravitate toward leaders who have a clear vision. Knowing "why we do these things around here" helps put management's expectations for individuals and teams into a meaningful context.

Authors James Kouzes and Barry Posner found that "when leaders effectively communicate a vision—whether it's to one person, a small group, or a large organization—that vision has very potent effects. We've found that when leaders clearly articulate their vision for the organization, constituents report significantly higher levels of the following:

- Job satisfaction
- Motivation
- Commitment
- Loyalty
- Esprit de corps
- Clarity about the organization's values
- Pride in the organization
- Organizational productivity

Clearly, teaching others about the vision produces powerful results."[7]

People want the best in themselves called out. They will rally around a communicated vision and work hard to support it. The vision also establishes a foundation of shared commitment and focus if and when times get rough.

Effective Team Goal Setting

What is a high-achievement goal? As we said earlier, studies show that high achievers set goals that they feel they have a 70 to 80 percent chance of accomplishing.

Some leaders feel you have to set goals that are almost unachievable just to keep people motivated and pushing harder. They would scoff at the idea of a goal that you had a 75 percent chance of accomplishing. However, research and our observation show that people will perform consistently the best and at a high level of accomplishment when the chances of success fall in that narrow window of 50 to 75 percent probability. If the goal has a greater than 75 percent chance of completion, high achievers (and most people) feel the goal is too easy. But high achievers want the publicly stated goal to be around that 75 percent range. Then, in their own minds, they will shoot for a much higher goal— one that they feel they may have only a fifty-fifty chance of accomplishing. They like this more-challenging goal because they feel it is their personal effort that will make the difference between the stated goal and this internal higher target.

But all studies show that once the stated goal has less than a fifty-fifty chance of success, it is no longer a motivating target. The chances of success are too slim.

We observed a fascinating example of this phenomenon when the leadership team for a client discussed the goal that had been publicly set by the CEO for them to accomplish over the next five years. We could tell by the team's discussion that they felt this goal was at or near the fifty-fifty odds range. While the goal seemed very challenging, there was a sense in the group that it might be attainable and the results would be exciting. But when one of the team members present indicated that the goal had recently been *increased* to accomplish about 30 percent more over the same five years, everyone in the room rolled their eyes, threw down their pens or pencils, and hung or shook their heads. The spirit went out of them. They obviously felt the new goal had less than a fifty-fifty chance of being achieved, and hope plummeted.

The moral of the story for leaders: Goal setting is very critical to future success, and a great deal of thought and feedback should be collected before announcing high-level goals. These goals may be broad goals stated to the public or to Wall Street. Or they may simply be individual goals that are set during annual review periods.

Team Feedback

The term *feedback* has an interesting origin. In the early days of rocketry, scientists found that in order to hit a target they had to devote more attention to building accurate, reliable, and frequent feedback mechanisms than they did to controlling thrust. Thrust was the easy part. Hitting the target was the hard part. It took feedback to maintain the ongoing focus required to achieve the goal.

Achievement in an organization is similar. Thrust is the easy part. You and others are willing to work long and hard to accomplish goals. However, as we've seen from the stories above, our efforts can become very scattered and focused on the "urgent." We need to build accurate, open, reliable feedback systems.

A team leader needs to create a learning environment in which every team member is appreciated, listened to, and respected. In this kind of environment, the opinions of team members are fully explored and understood and are incorporated into the decision-making process. The team actively learns from all members who express their positions and opinions, and as a result, the team is stronger and more efficient.

As you have seen from the outline of this book, the principles have an interesting pattern starting with humility and moving to endurance. In the end it will be the ability to endure through the challenges, criticisms, and doubts that distinguishes the great leaders. But if you have staked your reputation on a wrong or unachievable goal, enduring through the challenges will only take your team or organization down the wrong path. What keeps you from that wrong path is good solid feedback. But good solid feedback is hard to come by, especially the higher you climb in an organization. People don't like to give the boss bad news or news that doesn't agree with the boss's stated position. But without it comes only failure.

Feedback. It's not just something you ask for. It's a cherished gift. It's a wonderful reward for building a trusting organization or team.

An effective feedback apparatus starts with humility. Humble leaders create an atmosphere where feedback from others is desired and honestly requested. Leaders who are focused on growing their people build that growth on feedback. When people know that a leader is committed and wants honest feedback to help reach stated goals, they are more likely to provide the open and honest feedback required. Compassion, integrity, peacemaking—upcoming chapters that will all lead to an atmosphere and culture that is open to and thrives on honest and timely feedback.

Focus Together: An Exercise to Build Individual and Team Strength

The following chart, developed by Daniel Ofman,[8] and the corresponding exercise have been very successful in helping leaders identify core qualities (such as passion) and work through the pitfalls, challenges, and reactions to those core qualities. It is an effective way to help leaders examine themselves and then better understand how to maximize their core qualities. We have found that the exercise works best when done with a team.

- *Step 1: Core Quality.* Identify all the aspects of a specific core quality. For example, if passion is one of your core qualities, you may describe it as *exciting, adds energy, fires everyone up, contagious, overcomes obstacles, sees how things could be,* and so on. Select no more than one or two core qualities to examine. This step seeks to focus on your best core qualities.
- *Step 2: Pitfalls.* What happens when you get too much of a good thing? As is true for almost everyone, your strengths can become your Achilles heel. For example, what happens if you have too much passion? You could be driven, have tunnel vision, avoid reality, not accept failure or

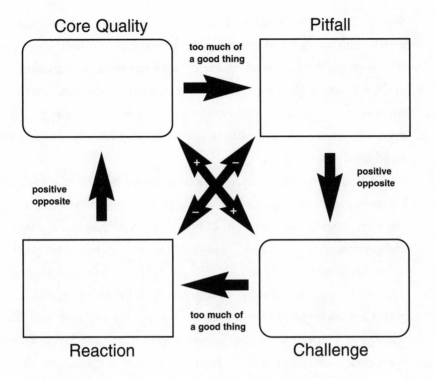

shortcomings, shy away from challenges, and so on. Therefore, we list all the pitfalls of passion in this step.

- *Step 3: Challenges.* What are some *positive* opposites of the pitfalls of your core quality? What are some positive actions you can take to avoid these pitfalls? For example, to address some of the pitfalls we listed above, you could ask a person or a team to function as a sounding board for you, setting specified times to check the reality of your situation. You could ask for and be open to challenges, or you could have another person or the whole team help you place your passion in the big picture of the organization. Look for positive opposites—ways to challenge and avoid the pitfalls and help yourself stay focused.

- *Step 4: Reaction.* What happens when you carry efforts to challenge your pitfalls too far? You may become discouraged and back away from your core quality. One reaction might be to not share your passion or to share it only with those who will not pose any challenges. Defensiveness or withdrawal are other reactions. This step will help you recognize your reactions and work to overcome your natural tendency to recoil under pressure.

A middle manager we know recently shared her concern with her supervisor about a program he wanted but that she believed might negatively impact the organization financially. She is a good manager and personally takes budgets and sales quotas to heart; it is her passion to hit the numbers every month. She also takes her job seriously and does not hesitate to speak up. In response to her criticism, the CEO pulled her aside and led her to believe that she was wrong in what she was saying. Her *reaction* to this confrontation was to say, "I'll just keep my mouth shut from now on!" Finding her passion threatened, she became discouraged by the CEO's remarks and wanted to avoid future confrontation. This woman's manager needs help finding some positive opposites to her *reaction* that will lead her back to her core quality.

The goal of this exercise is to help all team members stay in their positive balance, bouncing between their core qualities and their challenges rather than falling into the negative pattern of bouncing between their pitfalls and their reactions.

You can see from the arrows how this can happen. When played out in real-life situations, this chart is not a circle, but rather we move from corner to corner, either bouncing between our core qualities and challenges or bouncing between our pitfalls and reactions.

Finally, we draw your attention to the arrows between the boxes labeled "Too Much of a Good Thing." Notice that too much of the core quality leads to pitfalls, and too much working on the challenges leads to reactions. In either case, being out of balance leads to wrong behavior. Too much of anything leads us to a point of concern.

THE ESSENTIALS

- Just as every leader needs to clarify issues concerning personal passion and achievement, the team must undergo a similar process.
- Leaders must help the team identify the *important* versus the *urgent*. Does the team spend time and energy on the *important?*

Balancing Innovation and Execution

- Innovation is about execution—about getting things done.
- Competitive advantage is as much about execution as it is about strategy.
- A significant part of getting things done is focus.

The Achieving Team

- Organizations should channel resources into teaching leaders how to form realistic expectations, provide proper support, and establish achievable goals with appropriate incentives.
- *Energizing the team with vision*—People are hungry to be led and will gravitate toward leaders who have a clear vision.
- *Effective team goal setting*—Challenging but achievable goals should be set. Leaders need to be careful not to bury the team under unrealistic goals that have no team buy-in.

- *Team feedback*—It takes feedback to maintain the ongoing focus required to achieve a goal. Leaders need to build accurate, open, reliable feedback systems.

Focus Together

- The goal is to help all team members stay in their positive balance, bouncing between their core qualities and their challenges rather than falling into the negative pattern of bouncing between their pitfalls and their reactions.

CHANGE FROM THE INSIDE OUT

Good "music" is no accident! Team leaders are constantly listening to the "band" to determine whether the players are in tune, whether the rhythm is right. Do the individual sounds blend together for balance and harmony in the overall performance?

Modern-day bands wear headsets so they can listen intently to one another and cut out the unimportant noise around them. This allows them to give great feedback to one another and improve their performance. Solid feedback is essential to achieving a goal. Without it, you are not going to get where you want to go.

- How do people around you assume you would react to critical feedback?
- Do people shy away from giving you feedback? Do you get a limited amount of feedback?
- At the moment of truth, do you shy away from or soften feedback to others on the team?
- Do people come to you for straightforward, solid feedback?
- What can you do to build a team that uses open feedback for improving performance or team dynamics?

"Favored Are the Caring"

Compassion brings us to a stop, and for a moment
we rise above ourselves.

—MASON COOLEY, *City Aphorisms,* Twelfth Selection

D r. Albert Schweitzer was already an old man when Andrew C. Davison paid a visit to Schweitzer's jungle hospital in Lambaréné, on the banks of the Ogowe River in Gabon, Africa. The three-day visit had a deep and profound effect on Davison, who later wrote of one event during the trip that impressed him in a special way:

It was about eleven in the morning. The equatorial sun was beating down mercilessly, and we were walking up a hill with Dr. Schweitzer. Suddenly he left us and strode across the slope of the hill to a place where an African woman was struggling upward with a huge armload of wood for the cookfires. I watched with both admiration and concern as the eighty-five-year-old man took the entire load of wood and carried it on up the hill for the relieved woman. When we all reached the top of the hill, one of the members of our group asked Dr. Schweitzer why he did things like that, implying that in that heat and at his age he should not.

Albert Schweitzer, looking right at all of us and pointing to the woman, said simply, "No one should ever have to carry a burden like that alone."[1]

Schweitzer obviously understood compassion. As a leader he decided to care for someone else, to fully understand the woman's burden and seek to relieve it. In doing this he was supporting ideas taught by a compassionate Jesus who urged his followers to care for those who were hungry, sick, unclothed, in prison, and burdened with other problems—"Whatever you did for one of the least of these...you did for me."[2]

Compassion, as we define it here, involves two primary ideas: First is the ability to see people from their perspective, their level of interest, and their need. Coupled with that other-focused vision, though, is the deep internal craving to help them gain their full potential.

J. Oswald Sanders wrote,

> The true leader regards the welfare of others rather than his own comfort and prestige as of primary concern. He manifests sympathy and concern for those under him in their problems, difficulties, and cares, but it is a sympathy that fortifies and stimulates, not that softens and weakens.[3]

That's what we want to make sure is understood in this section: Compassion is a strong character quality that seeks to both understand people and motivate them to great personal and professional achievement. Compassion should not be confused with weak sentimentality. Instead, compassion involves caring strength, a selfless desire, and energy that elevates others to first place in all human affairs.

10

"I Care"

One day a student asked anthropologist Margaret Mead for the earliest sign of civilization in a given culture. He expected the answer to be a clay pot or perhaps a fishhook or grinding stone. Her answer was "a healed femur." Mead explained that no healed femurs are found where the law of the jungle, the survival of the fittest, reigns. A healed femur shows that someone cared. Someone had to hunt and gather for the injured person until the leg healed. That caring evidence of compassion, according to Mead, is the first sign of civilization.

Great leaders demonstrate such caring. This expression is more than empathy or a heart for the needy. It is a compelling conviction to care enough to become involved and help others by taking some action that will improve their lives or set them on a fresh course.

QUALITIES THAT DEMONSTRATE CARING

The following qualities characterize a leader who says in words and actions, "I care."

Understanding

We need to be acutely aware of other people's needs, focus, dreams, and abilities before we can help them achieve.

For years the late cartoonist Charles Schulz delighted us as his Peanuts characters Charlie Brown, Linus, and even Snoopy provided a window into the complex (and funny) realm of human relations.

Lucy, the extroverted big sister of Linus, was no exception. Her love affair with the Beethoven-loving Schroeder is legendary. Often we see Lucy stretched out by Schroeder's piano, watching him with longing eyes. Or she is asking a question or demanding his attention in some other way. Schroeder is oblivious to Lucy, so she tries harder and harder to win his heart. In the end, nothing works. Lucy usually loses her temper and pouts, once again the frustrated lover.

What Lucy never gets is how a change in her approach might improve her chances at winning Schroeder's attention. Lucy's entire focus is on *her* needs, not Schroeder's. Every attempt to secure the heart of the piano genius is from her perspective, not his. Her compassion is entirely self-focused and has little or nothing to do with him and his needs. No matter how bold or romantic she is, Lucy never gets close to Schroeder because she never learns to first understand him.

Increased understanding of others usually leads to better relationships. Our frame of reference becomes *their needs,* not our own. It becomes a habit to seek to understand our bosses, our direct-reports, and our peers. This understanding is not developed for manipulative purposes. It is an attempt to help people grow and develop by first seeking to understand them—their motives, needs, and styles. Once we understand others and their individual preferences, we can better communicate with them, train them, and lead them.

Abraham Lincoln was a master at this. In 1864 the *New York Herald* explained how Lincoln was able to overcome the difficulties of guiding the nation during the Civil War—"Plain common sense, a kindly disposition, a straight forward purpose, and a shrewd perception of the ins and outs of poor, weak human nature."

Lincoln was a master at getting out to meet and know the people—from generals to office workers: "Lincoln gained commitment and respect from his people because he was willing to take time out from his busy schedule to hear what his people had to say."[1] From this information, Lincoln came to understand his people. From this understanding, he motivated them, challenged them, and moved them to achieve.

It is always interesting, upon entering an airplane, to look into the cockpit and see all those dials and gauges. Each one has a purpose. Many help properly guide the aircraft to its final destination. If the pilots don't monitor the right instruments, they won't have a clear picture of the flight, where they are going, how fast they are traveling, how high they are flying, or even if the craft is right side up.

Similarly, if we do not read all the "gauges" of other people, we will be forced to guess what their behavior and words really mean. Learning to read gauges gives you the ability to understand and respond to others based on their needs and frames of reference.

Concern

Another quality of a caring leader is a concern for others. The good Samaritan demonstrated concern: "He went to him [the beaten and robbed stranger] and bandaged his wounds, pouring on oil and wine. Then he put the man on his own donkey, took him to an inn and took care of him."[2] The good Samaritan showed compassion and sincere concern for the robbery victim he found beside the road. He did not hesitate. He moved quickly, then took the time necessary to give the man attention. This is sincere concern.

The axiom says "I don't care how much you know until I know how much you care." When you really care, people know it and will respond positively to your efforts to help them flourish.

Caring in Action

Caring becomes real to another person only when some action occurs. We believe that communication, confrontation, and challenge are three of the best ways a leader puts "feet" to true caring.

Communication. The groundbreaking book *In Search of Excellence* stressed the concept known as MBWA, "management by walking around." The concept is taken further in the book *A Passion for Excellence:*

> How good are you? No better than your people and their commitment and participation in the business as full partners, and as business people. The fact that you get them all together to share whatever—results, experiences, recent small successes and the like—at least once every couple of weeks seems to us to be a small price indeed to pay for that commitment and sense of teamwork and family. The "return on investment" is probably far and away the best of any program in the organization.[3]

MBWA stresses getting out of our individual comfort zones and getting to know other people. Whether you attend company-wide meetings or individual private sessions, the lesson is clear: Get out of your office and communicate with your people.

We tend to assume that communication is merely the process of delivering information from one person to another. However, it is much more than just good delivery. Pat Williams writes,

> Communication is a process by which we build relationships and trust, share meaning and values and feelings, and transcend the aloneness and isolation of being distinct, individual souls. Communication is not just a data dump. Communication is connection.[4]

How we express ourselves positively or negatively affects our listeners. The message intertwines with the messenger. More sobering is the fact that listeners may never hear our message because it is not in a form they appreciate.

Communication means being connected with your people. It means getting out of your office into their offices and workspaces.

Confrontation. Part of leading is confronting people and urging them toward better performance.

It was a classic match-up. Twenty-game winner "The Rocket" Roger Clemens took the hill for the World Champion New York Yankees in game seven of the 2001 World Series against 22-game winner, Curt Schilling, the Arizona Diamondbacks' ace.

This was not the first time they had squared off. In the winter of 1991, Clemens noticed Schilling working out in an adjacent weight room at the Astrodome. The 28-year-old Clemens asked the younger 24-year-old Schilling if they could talk. Schilling thought it would be cool to talk some baseball with Clemens, but he had no idea what Clemens had on his mind.

Clemens proceeded to get in Schilling's face, telling him he wasn't taking advantage of the gifts God had given him and as a result wasn't respecting himself, his teammates, or the game.

According to Clemens the conversation got heated, but it had an impact on Schilling: "I walked away saying to myself, (1) why would he care as much as he did? and, (2) if he did care, there must be something there."

Schilling says, "I began to turn a corner at that point in my career, both on and off the field."

Neither pitcher won that seventh game of the world series (Randy Johnson of the Diamondbacks did), but game seven must have been a proud day for Clemens—first, because he pitched well, but second, because someone whom he cared enough about to confront ten years earlier had pitched just as well.[5]

Confrontation does not involve giving a report on another person's behavior. It means offering feedback on the other's role or response. Its goal, in the business environment, is to bring the employee, boss, or peer face to face with issues (behavior, emotions, achievement) that are being avoided.

For us to be effective in confrontation, we need to focus on four things:

1. Balanced truth. You cannot confront someone on hearsay alone. Get the facts. Investigate the matter; check it out. There are always two sides to every story. What are they? Neither one is likely to be the "complete" truth. Look for the balanced story.

2. Right timing. We recently witnessed a near catastrophe. A client of ours was going to confront a customer. The customer had called the day before and verbally leveled several people on our friend's staff. Our client was going to call the customer and confront him with some brutal truth: "Everyone in the office is afraid of you and doesn't want to talk to you because of your aggressive style and attitude." Just before our client was to make the call, someone in the office discovered that the customer's wife had colon cancer and possibly multiple sclerosis. The customer was suffering right along with his wife, in addition to trying to be both Dad and Mom to the kids, coaching a sports team, and running a tough business. Instead of calling to confront the customer with the brutal facts, our client decided to confront him with care and sympathy.

Many situations will not be this clear-cut. The right timing may be harder to gauge. For sure, though, it is best to deal with a situation when the heat of the moment has passed. Having the courage and taking the time to come back to it after emotions have subsided is actually quite difficult. There never seems to be the same urgency later, but good leaders force themselves to pick up the issue at a better moment. When it is the right time to confront, the green lights will be flashing. Until then, hold on.

3. Wise wording. We suggest that you carefully plan what you will say when you confront someone. A proverb says, "Timely advice is as lovely as golden apples in a silver basket. Valid criticism is as treasured by the one who heeds it as jewelry made from finest gold."[6] Words have the power to destroy or heal. Choose them carefully when confronting.

4. Fearless courage. Don't fall back in fear when you need to confront someone. If you have assembled the truth, believe it is the right moment, and have carefully prepared what you will say, move forward and confront. As Roger Clemens did with Curt Schilling, press on: "How can I help this person be better, regardless of how I feel?" It may mean finding a more productive or satisfying place for the person—even if it's with another company. In the end this option is better for the organization and, in most cases, for the other person. What is worse is allowing a person to continue in a harmful behavior or self-destructive attitude.

Challenge. An often overlooked aspect of compassion is the desire to help a person grow. Compassion includes challenging others to attain high-quality results on projects that stretch them. People need challenge in their lives, and leaders need to help their employees see the value of it not only for their own well-being but for the well-being of the organization as well.

Some years ago I (Wayne) was asked to tackle an impossible task. I assumed leadership for a company division that had underperformed for several years. I inherited a group of salespeople whose only motivation was retirement. In addition, the division was overstocked with wrong inventory, and customer complaints were stacked high.

I rolled up my sleeves and began working to pull the department together. The first goal was our sales team. Together we worked out some new incentive programs and some additional benefits *if* sales quotas were met. Then we turned our attention to the customers, and, one by one, we solved their problems, creating a renewed commitment to service within the division. Next came sales and marketing strategies. With the team's help, we launched a new marketing campaign that began to increase sales. We aggressively sold off the old inventory and partnered with a supplier to provide us with fresh stock from his facility. We were on a roll!

In three months sales and profits were up, and the crew (all but one stayed with the program) was happy and productive.

One day my boss put his arm around my shoulders and asked me if I was aware that I had accomplished what many thought was impossible. He asked me what I had learned from the experience and told me, "I'm sorry for all the extra work the last few months. I hope you understand—I did this to help you grow into a better manager."

This man challenged me to be better. His desire was to help me grow by throwing me into the middle of an almost impossible situation. Sure, the company prospered, but his goal also included my personal growth and development.

Spontaneous Compassion

We observed a wonderful incident of compassion once while preparing a Webcast for a client. The man helping set up the equipment and handling the technical details received a telephone call from one of his employees who was troubleshooting at another location. We learned that this employee was working on a crisis situation of great importance to her company.

Hearing just half of his conversation, we picked up that she was reporting on her progress in solving the problem. Later, when our technical helper gave us the details of the conversation, we learned that almost in passing she mentioned, "I have to check on my father. I think he had a heart attack or stroke or something."

Our man interrupted the conversation right then and said bluntly, "You need to go to your father." He didn't even ask, "Do you need to go to your father?" He just said, "You need to go to your father."

The employee protested, "No, I'm not going to go until this is fixed." Her boss just kept saying, "Get off the phone, get on a plane, and go to your father."

We knew that this man might get into trouble for making that kind of decision; his employee was trying to solve a serious problem. But he insisted, and she went home.

We reach several conclusions from this leader's act of spontaneous compassion: First, this woman will be one of his most loyal and productive employees from now on. Second, he did the right thing even though painful consequences might follow. A trusted leader acts like that. Finally, he showed a true heart of compassion. He decided to care for the person. In that moment when he had to make a choice, he understood and responded to the needs of the person, not just a valued cog in the company machine.

That's what compassion is all about.

THE ESSENTIALS

- Compassion is a compelling conviction to care enough to become involved and help others by taking some action that will improve their lives or set them on a fresh course.

QUALITIES THAT DEMONSTRATE CARING

- *Understanding*—Leaders need to be acutely aware of other people's needs, focus, dreams, and abilities before they can help their people achieve.

- *Concern*—The good Samaritan did not hesitate. He moved quickly, then took the time necessary to give the hurt man attention. This is sincere concern.
- *Caring in action*—Communication, confrontation, and challenge are three of the best ways a leader puts "feet" to true caring.
  1. *Communication*—Get out of your office and communicate with your people. "Communication is connection."
  2. *Confrontation*—This does not involve giving a report on another person's behavior. Its goal, in the business environment, is to bring the employee, boss, or peer face to face with issues (behavior, emotions, achievement) that are being avoided.
  3. *Challenge*—Compassion includes challenging others to attain high-quality results on projects that stretch them.

SPONTANEOUS COMPASSION

- Effective leaders act spontaneously with a true heart of compassion, caring for the person regardless of the consequences.

CHANGE FROM THE INSIDE OUT

"I don't care how much you know until I know how much you care."

Many leaders believe they must completely separate their work life from their personal life. Many of them will say, "I don't dare get too close to these people because I won't be able to be objective if I need to give them critical feedback."

But people follow leaders who care. People know they care, and they develop trust. If you are a caring, honestly challenging leader, people will follow you through the tough course of business ups and downs.

- Would your people say they really know you? If not, why not?
- Have you developed caring relationships anywhere in your life, or have you kept everyone, even your family, at arm's length? Explain.
- What concerns do you have about your ability to be a good leader if you let others know that you care and allow them to care for you?

"You First"

Compassion is not easy or cheap. A leader who sincerely seeks to understand and care for others will pay a price. But the rewards are satisfying and great.

This chapter will examine compassion from the perspective of a "you-first" leader—the man or woman whose focus is on responding to the needs of employees, customers, and community before his or her own needs.

We urge you to be a person and leader known for radical acts of compassion. Here's an incredible example:

It was 1944, and Bert Frizen was an infantryman on the front lines in Europe. American forces had advanced in the face of intermittent shelling and small-arms fire throughout the morning hours, but now all was quiet. His patrol reached the edge of a wooded area with an open field before them. Unknown to the Americans, a battery of Germans waited in a hedgerow about two hundred yards across the field.

Bert was one of two scouts who moved out into the clearing. Once he was halfway across the field, the remainder of his battalion followed. Suddenly, the Germans opened fire, and machine gun fire ripped into both of Bert's legs. The American battalion withdrew into the woods for protection, while a rapid exchange of fire continued.

Bert lay helplessly in a small stream as shots volleyed overhead. There seemed to be no way out. To make matters worse, he now noticed that a German soldier was crawling toward him. Death appeared imminent; he closed his eyes and waited. To his surprise, a considerable period passed without the expected attack, so he ventured opening his eyes again. He was startled to see the German kneeling at his side, smiling. He then noticed that the shooting had stopped. Troops from both sides of the battlefield watched anxiously. Without any verbal exchange, this mysterious German reached down to lift Bert in his arms and proceeded to carry him to the safety of Bert's comrades.

Having accomplished his self-appointed mission, and still without speaking a word, the German soldier turned and walked back across the field to his own troop. No one dared break the silence of this sacred moment. Moments later the cease-fire ended, but not before all those present had witnessed how one man risked everything for his enemy.[1]

How would your business, your family, your community—our world—be better if more of these radical acts of compassion occurred on a daily basis?

We can respond with compassion to every person we encounter by thinking "you first." Jesus constantly demonstrated this approach with his team of disciples. Perhaps the most memorable example occurred shortly before his death when he got down on his knees and washed their feet. In this humbling act he demonstrated to them that even as their leader he desired to serve them. He wanted them to understand that in his view—the ultimate leader—the needs of others came first.

An entire, well-established management perspective has evolved from this concept of service to others. Robert K. Greenleaf first used the term *servant leadership* in a 1970 essay.

This is a very counterintuitive notion in our day when competition is fierce in nearly every area of life. You can't "look out for number 1" and say "you first" at the same time. So then how do we learn to put others first?

CHARACTERISTICS OF A "YOU-FIRST" LEADER

One way to find out whether a leader has a "you-first" perspective is to ask, Do others grow as individuals under this person's leadership? While benefiting from this leader's compassion, do others become healthier, wiser, freer, more autonomous, and more likely themselves to develop a "you-first" attitude?

We believe the following qualities define a leader who is committed to being last rather than first:

1. Commitment to the growth of people. In their book *The Leadership Challenge,* James Kouzes and Barry Posner write, "Any leadership practice that increases another's sense of self-confidence, self-determination, and personal effectiveness makes that person more powerful and greatly enhances the possibility of success."[2]

Author Alan Loy McGinnis observed, "There is no more noble occupation in the world than to assist another human being—to help someone succeed." A commitment to growing people is not a temporary fix, a quick solution to a problem, or a short-term shot in the arm that helps them only today. Commitment to growth is a long-term investment in other people. It increases their opportunities to grow, learn, and use what they have learned to its greatest benefit. When their growth multiplies, the organization's growth and maturity multiplies.

2. Listening. As we discussed earlier, good leaders are too often viewed as being great verbal communicators and decision makers. While these attributes are important, leaders need to expand their leadership style to include a deep commitment to listening to others. How can an effective leader understand the needs of his or her employees, customers, suppliers, or market without listening

139

intently to them? Psychologist Dr. Joyce Brothers remarked, "Listening, not imitation, may be the sincerest form of flattery."

Listening can be difficult for any leader. I (Wayne) worked with an entrepreneur who had carved out an extremely successful manufacturing business. He was a hard worker, and he expected his people to work hard as well. His belief was that his success came from his ideas, his money, his way of doing things.

When it was time for a new computer system to be installed, I helped him find the software solution and the hardware and began to plan the installation and training. He wanted the main processor to be in a certain room of the building. I advised against it. The room was located too close to the area where he machined parts. I was afraid that the fine metal dust created from the lathes would hurt the system. We discussed it, and I thought I had convinced him, between phone interruptions, to put the CPU some other place.

A week later I received a phone call while at another client's location. It was the owner of the manufacturing company. He told me to drop everything and come to his office. He screamed into the phone, "That computer you told us to buy is no good. It's been here only one week, and it keeps shutting down!"

When I arrived at the office, the administrative staff seemed scared to death. The owner was on a rampage. He pulled me into the room that I had advised against, and there was the CPU. I looked at it, and the area in front of the cooling fans was filthy. Employees had left the outer door open in the office, and as he had been warned, tiny metal shavings had invaded the processor and disk drives. The system was ruined.

This man was not a listener, and it cost him not only a computer system but his company. A few years later, despite warnings from his financial people and the bank, he went out of business. He just had to do things his way—a way that did not include listening to others.

What made a difference for me (Ron) was when I finally grasped the concept of listening with the intent to *understand*. I had always listened with the intent to *respond*. The entire time I was listening, my mind was developing responses, recording counterpoints, cataloging quick points that I was sure the other person would find helpful when I responded. Listening with the intent to respond is not compassionate. It is not humble. It's self-focused. Listening with the intent to understand is indeed focused on the other person.

As I work with leaders and spend time listening with the intent to understand, I'm amazed at how much they are willing to share with me when they know I fully intend not to just hear them but also to understand.

3. Awareness. Both self-awareness and general awareness direct leaders to better understand situations and people. Robert Greenleaf wrote,

> Awareness is not a giver of solace—it is just the opposite. It is a disturber and an awakener. Able leaders are usually sharply awake and reasonably disturbed. They are not seekers after solace. They have their own inner serenity.[3]

Awareness helps leaders discern how to properly put others first.

4. Empathy. This is identifying with and understanding another's situation, feelings, and motives. People need to know they are accepted and recognized for their special gifts and talents.

John was the head of a large entertainment company. He was concerned about everything but his employees and their needs. He lacked many of the qualifications of a great leader, but one of his most glaring deficiencies was empathy. Whenever an employee (executive, manager, or worker) expressed some personal problem or work-related difficulty, John would immediately take that as a cue to either go into his own personal problems or tell the employee, manager, or executive how deficient the person was in his or her job. John made a lot of money, so most employees could not imagine that he could have any of the same problems they experienced. That didn't matter to John. He just went right into his monologue. Over time, he lost all of his good employees and leaders. The company, now a shadow of its former self, is simply "getting by."

5. *Healing.* One of the greatest assets of a "you-first" leader is the ability to approach another person as a healer in a spirit of help and compassion.

When she first came to work, Diana was hardly a candidate for employee of the year. In fact, because she had made some terrible choices as a teenager, she was in pain and carrying a load of personal baggage. But the "you-first" manager she reported to sensed that beyond Diana's broken spirit was a person loaded with raw talent and drive. But first some negatives needed attention. Diana had gaps in her formal training. So the manager worked with Diana on a plan to bring her to a place of peak performance. As she experienced some modest success early on and began getting rid of self-doubts and limiting habits, Diana blossomed. Soon her progress was exponential. Her manager tailored a bonus plan for Diana. She did so well that she outran the plan, creating a financial strain on the manager's budget!

To this day Diana continues to thrive in both her professional and personal life. All of that started with a manager who could look beyond his own needs and place another person first. His commitment to healing opened the door for Diana to walk through and enjoy her job and her life.

6. *Persuasion over power.* Many times when a job is hard to do, poor leaders rely on sheer power rather than persuasion. The compassionate leader seeks to engage others rather than force compliance. There's a desire to build consensus rather than use authoritarian power. Jesus told compelling stories called parables to help people see that what he was saying was not only different but also better for them. His disciples were confused. Why didn't he just use his power and "force" people to believe? Jesus knew that he was much better off helping people understand through noncoercive means. With their consensus

came the real power to accomplish something great. Power trips and plays deflate people and do not allow them to think for themselves.

This list of six characteristics of a "you-first" leader is by no means exhaustive, but each quality is fundamental if you want compassion to be a key component of your leadership style.

THE REWARDS

Becoming a "you-first" leader may sound a bit like career suicide. Isn't this just another way to get trampled while climbing the corporate ladder? While this can happen, there are actually great personal and professional rewards awaiting the person intent on taking care of the needs of others *first*. In the long run compassion, like humility, will be an asset that will propel you into being an admired leader, one whom others will follow. It will also provide you with a great deal of personal satisfaction and delight.

Having a "you-first" attitude will result in a new and better personal leadership paradigm. Instead of viewing employees and others as those in need of control and reshaping, you will move toward becoming a coach who provides people with honest feedback. You will create a safe environment in which people are free to share honestly about your programs, ideas, vision, and initiatives.

Another way to look at yourself and develop good habits is to examine whether you act as an old-style boss, or whether your actions (not intentions, but real actions) are directed toward empowering others.

The following table, modified from the original work done by Ann McGee-Cooper,[4] Ed.D., author of *Time Management for Unmanageable People* and *You Don't Have to Go Home from Work Exhausted*, explores the differences between the "boss as judge" and the "you-first" leader.

Though simple in concept, being a leader who puts his or her people first is difficult to put into practice. It takes time, energy, commitment, patience, and

BOSS AS JUDGE OVER EMPLOYEE	"YOU-FIRST" LEADER
• Top-down. • Boss controls "when," "how," and even "if."	• Two-way communication with people. • Teamwork, open flow of ideas.
• Reactive. Punishment/reward system. • Accountability is a "have to."	• Proactive. Celebration. Failing forward. • Accountability is a "want to" or a "get to."
• Seen as judging. • Win or lose. • Based on distrust.	• Seen as learning. • Goal is win/win/win. • Based on trust.
• Legalistic. Monitor. • Expectations fixed.	• Holistic. Mentor relationship. • Expectations in constant flux (growth and change anticipated).
• Accountability as an excuse/ justification.	• Accountability as dialogue to raise the level of "collective intelligence."
• Extrinsically driven.	• Intrinsically driven.

a host of other self-sacrificing qualities. That's the price. However, putting others first does work. This way of showing compassion will create an environment where top performance is possible. And you will experience great personal satisfaction as you watch people grow, learn, stretch, and become "you-first" leaders themselves.

Our hope is that you will embark on this journey of putting others first. It may take a lifetime to get this "right," but you will never regret it.

THE ESSENTIALS

- The "you-first" leader is the man or woman whose focus is on responding to the needs of employees, customers, and community before his or her own needs.

CHARACTERISTICS OF A "YOU-FIRST" LEADER

- *Commitment to the growth of people*—This is a long-term investment in other people.
- *Listening*—Leaders need to expand their leadership style to include a deep commitment to listening to others.
- *Awareness*—Great leaders are usually "sharply awake and reasonably disturbed." This helps them discern how to properly put others first.
- *Empathy*—People need to know they are accepted and recognized for their special gifts and talents.
- *Healing*—One of the greatest assets of a "you-first" leader is the ability to approach another person as a healer in a spirit of help and compassion.
- *Persuasion over power*—The compassionate leader seeks to engage others rather than force compliance.

THE REWARDS

- Having a "you-first" attitude will result in a new and better personal leadership paradigm.
- "You-first" leaders create a safe environment in which people are free to share honestly about their programs, ideas, vision, and initiatives.

CHANGE FROM THE INSIDE OUT

Are you the kind of person who believes in the "fixed pie" view of the world? "There is only so much pie to go around, so if I don't get mine first, there won't be any left after everyone takes theirs." Or do you believe in an expanding pie? "If we all do a great job, there will be more than enough to go around for all of us." "You first."

Zig Ziglar has built a whole career based on the concept that to get everything you want you need to help other people get what they want. "You first."

A "you-first" leadership style goes beyond humility. Humility says, "I'm no better than you; we are equally important." A "you-first" attitude puts the other person out front.

- How much are your decisions driven by your own selfishness?
- What are you trying to protect by not seeking a "you-first" style when you work with others?
- Have you ever experienced personal satisfaction by putting another person first, placing their needs ahead of your own? Explain.

"Favored Are Those with Unshakable Ethics"

The man who tries to walk two roads will split his pants.

—AFRICAN PROVERB

n their book *Credibility: How Leaders Gain and Lose It, Why People Demand It,* James Kouzes and Barry Posner surveyed thousands of people across this country and around the world. In the process they completed over four hundred written case studies. As they identified characteristics most people desire in a leader, honesty or integrity was identified more frequently than any other trait.[1]

That seems to make perfect sense. People are most willing to follow someone they can trust. They want to know that leaders will be straight with them, will be consistent, will follow through on what they say, and will be true to a set of values.

So what has happened to us? As we write this book, corporate America is hurting. Never before have so many executives been under investigation, and never before have so many not been trusted. *USA Today* reports,

> More than seven in 10 Americans say they distrust CEOs of large corporations. Nearly eight in 10 believe that top executives of large companies will take "improper actions" to help themselves at the expense of their

companies. In the past nine months, the percentage of Americans who say they see Big Business as an actual threat to the nation's future has nearly doubled, to 38%.[2]

This lack of trust seems to have resulted from a corporate culture in which leaders have shown a complete disregard for personal integrity.

BusinessWeek Online reported that on February 7, 1999, the audit committee of Enron Corporation's board of directors heard the company auditors describe Enron's accounting practices as "high risk." In response, none of the directors objected to the procedures, requested a second opinion, or demanded more prudent measures. Further, a Senate subcommittee investigation found that similar reports by Arthur Andersen personnel occurred once or twice each year from 1999 through 2001 with the same result: Not one director drilled deep enough into the details or objected to the high-risk practices.[3]

Building trust with employees, peers, and investors starts and ends with integrity. Consciously or subconsciously, all leaders decide what values to adopt. Either they choose truth, honesty, and fairness or they choose "cooking the books," "image managing," and winning at all costs.

If integrity is so important to people, why don't our leaders seek to live it? Is it a quality you seek in your own life? If people do not believe your words or if they doubt the credibility of your actions, how will you accomplish anything of value? Who will take you seriously?

Jesus said that "where your treasure is, there your heart will be also."[4]

Integrity represents a great treasure. Seek it with all your heart.

The Real Deal

The root word for *integrity* is *integer*—a whole or complete number. Leaders who focus on integrity chose to live a "whole" life.

Of course, they won't do it perfectly, but in spite of normal and expected human frailties, a principled leader strives to be whole, undivided. He or she is "the real deal."

C. William Pollard wrote in *The Soul of the Firm*,

As we seek to understand and apply a cause for our work, our desire is not to be known for what we know but for what we do. We must be people of integrity seeking to do that which is right even when no one is looking and staying committed whether the test is adversity or prosperity.[1]

Yes, that's exactly it. *Integrity.*

BARRIERS TO INTEGRITY

Becoming a "whole" leader is more easily contemplated than accomplished. Before we explore the attitudes and actions that build a life of integrity, let's first take a look at several stumbling blocks that are not always easily seen or sur-mounted on the journey.

Fear

Anyone called into the principal's office in elementary school understands the fear associated with integrity. Do I tell the truth? Do I keep my friends out of trouble? What will happen to us if I tell the principal exactly what we did?

If we do not combat fear, a downward spiral begins. Fearful thoughts lead to paralysis. President Harry S. Truman once said,

> The worst danger we face is the danger of being paralyzed by doubts and fears. This danger is brought on by those who abandon faith and sneer at hope. It is brought on by those who spread cynicism and distrust and try to blind us to the great chance to do good for all mankind.[2]

When we are paralyzed by fear, we tend to lose perspective and often make decisions or act in ways that do not support our integrity. Fear-caused paraly-sis then leads to procrastination.

Fear does tend to immobilize. Victor Kiam once said, "Procrastination is opportunity's natural assassin." Our people, the project, and the organization wait for us to act, and we cannot. When they observe our inaction, people begin to wonder what is so important about the assignment or initiative. Our lack of action sends a powerful—if unintended—message: Our actions (or resulting inactions) do not match our intentions.

Finally, as we hit bottom in this fear spiral, procrastination leads to pur-poselessness. We find ourselves losing our vision and hope. We vacillate and lose heart. We are paralyzed, we procrastinate, and then we simply give up. Integrity and living a life of quality sink below our radar. We expect—or others expect us—to deliver results, but we are bound by such fear that we lose our sense of direction and, along the way, our core strength.

Compromise

Compromising values happens gradually over time—one little lie or indiscretion adds to another until, almost imperceptibly, integrity and character erode. Finally, at some point our integrity is overwhelmed.

A friend of ours once said, "Sin always takes you farther than you intend to go and keeps you longer than you intend to stay." Compromising our integrity leads to a similar situation.

We wrote in an earlier chapter about a person who, in his arrogance, compromised his marriage and career because of multiple affairs. His exploits didn't just happen all at once; they occurred over time. A little "innocent" flirting later turns into a date, then a date turns into an affair. Most people don't just plunge into compromising situations. It happens one step at a time.

Many of the business tragedies we are living through today started as minor omissions or small wrong decisions. Over time they grew, and suddenly the CEOs found themselves telling lies to their stockholders, employees, and the media. Records were fudged; fortunes have been lost. And it all started with one small compromise.

Hypocrisy

Sir Francis Bacon once wrote, "A bad man is worse when he pretends to be a saint." An old Chinese proverb adds, "It is difficult to have each foot in a separate boat." Hypocrisy, like fear and compromise, can destroy integrity and render leaders trustless.

The word *hupokrisis* was used in classical Greek as part of theatrical acting. It came to mean acting a part. In this sense the greatest actors are true hypocrites: They assume a role and act out a part. Their acting roles are separate from their real lives.

But in leadership, integrity is about actions matching beliefs. Do leaders "act" the part or are they genuine? Does their walk match their talk?

We once worked with a company where the CEO played many "parts." In fact, he played so many parts that on many days the employees could not uncover who he really was. He was one person to the stockholders, another to his direct-reports, and a third person to employees (when he chose to speak to them). He would talk eloquently at company meetings about teamwork but work hard behind the scenes to create fear and tension between the divisions. He would promise profits to the shareholders but make wasteful decisions that eroded profits and cash flow. Eventually he left the company, but the wake of his hypocrisy nearly bankrupted the organization.

Fear, compromise, and hypocrisy are daunting barriers to a life of integrity. But living the alternative—a whole life of integrity—is definitely possible and well worth the effort.

A Life of Integrity

Before Peter Parker—the superhero Spider-Man—went public with his new-found superpowers, he had a heart-to-heart conversation with his Uncle Ben. Sitting in the car, Uncle Ben admonished, "These are the years when a man becomes the man he's going to be for the rest of his life. Just be careful who you change into. You're feeling this great power, and with great power comes great responsibility."[3]

Although these are fictional characters, Uncle Ben's advice was sound: *Be careful what you become.*

Stephen Covey's insights on staying consistent to a vision are well known but deserve repetition. He writes:

> [To] "begin with the end in mind" is to begin today with the image,
> picture, or paradigm of the end of your life as your frame of reference or
> the criterion by which everything else is examined.... By keeping that
> end clearly in mind, you can make certain that whatever you do on any

particular day does not violate criteria you have defined as supremely important, and that each day of your life contributes in a meaningful way to the vision you have of your life as a whole.[4]

Peter Drucker describes the "mirror test" in which leaders make sure that the person they see in the mirror in the morning is the kind of person they want to be, the kind of person they can respect and believe in.[5] If there is a lack of consistency between our public and private lives, then eventually we will be unable to manage the divide. Integrity will crumble. We read of far too many leaders who have fallen as the truth about their private lives has emerged.

Living a "whole" life means doing things in a way that is consistent with our values and vision. It means standing firm on tough issues and making difficult choices. In a word, it means *integrity*. Here are three ways to reach that goal.

1. Act boldly. Bold acts issue from a person who has unshakable confidence. That confidence comes from knowing the principles that guide your life and knowing that these principles will lead to integrity.

It is important to know the values and principles that drive your behavior. Only then will you have the confidence to act boldly in spite of peer pressure or prevailing opinions.

Leaders who want a total quality life seek to act boldly when faced with compromising decisions and actions. They have no fear because they fall back on their values and their deep need to live a life of integrity and trust.

2. Exhibit a great attitude. Another path to integrity as a "whole" existence is to approach all you do with a joyful, positive, uplifting mind-set. The pursuit of integrity requires what is best and noble in your character. You can't afford the defeating, polluting influence of a negative outlook.

Performance specialist Dr. Bob Rotella writes about golf, yet his insights translate to leadership as well: "Standing on the tee and thinking about your drive going to the target doesn't guarantee that it will go there. It only enhances the chances. [By contrast] Negative thinking is almost 100 percent effective."[6]

To succeed in business or any other challenge, we must maintain a great attitude. No matter what the obstacle or opposition, successful leaders believe they can overcome and win the battle. Their mind-set influences their performance, and there is no substitute for a positive outlook.

Understandably, it is hard to have a positive perspective when we are weighed down by doubts about our own character. When we're one person in the mirror and another person to our employees, we're divided and out of sync. When we—or others—question our integrity, it's difficult to not allow doubt to overshadow our attitude and performance.

3. *Develop trust.* Integrity and trust are interwoven like two strands in a tightly wound cord. It's really impossible to have one quality without the other. How do you become a person others trust?

In the organizational setting in particular, trustworthiness is based on both character—what you are—and competence—how well you do what you do. It is quite possible to have one quality and not the other. If you have confidence in my character but consider me woefully incompetent at my job, you may like me but not trust me.

Stephen Covey again:

Trustworthiness is the foundation of trust. Trust is the emotional bank account between two people, which enables two parties to have a win-win performance agreement. If two people trust each other, based on the trustworthiness of each other, they can then enjoy clear communication, empathy, synergy, and productive interdependency. If one is incompetent, training and development can help. But if one has a character flaw, he or she must make and keep promises to increase internal security, improve skills, and rebuild relationships of trust. Trust or the lack of it is at the root of the success or failure in relationships and in the bottom-line results of business, industry, education, and government.[7]

Trustworthy people are dependable and consistent; their actions and lifestyles set an example of integrity and competence.

Robert Cooper summarized trust so powerfully:

Trust is an emotional strength that begins with a feeling of self-worth and purpose that we're called to extend outward to others. The warm, solid gut feeling you get from trust—from counting on yourself and trusting and being trusted by others—is one of the great enablers of life. With it, we have the inner room to grow, to become emotionally fit, and to exercise and expand our capacity to build bridges from one issue to another, one idea to another, one person to another.[8]

Building trust takes time. We can trust others and gain their trust when certain qualities are present, but we also need to remember that years of baggage associated with our personal lives, our leadership style, and how we do things can get in the way. Therefore, patience and understanding become necessary allies as we sort through our lives and seek to trust others.

Integrity and the trust it births are a leader's treasured assets to be guarded at all costs. It is difficult to build an organization—or a life—successfully without integrity.

With integrity, you're the real deal.

THE ESSENTIALS

- People are most willing to follow someone they can trust. The current lack of trust in business leadership seems to have resulted from a corporate culture in which leaders have shown a complete disregard for personal integrity.
- Building trust with employees, peers, and investors starts and ends with integrity.

BARRIERS TO INTEGRITY

- *Fear*—Fearful thoughts lead to paralysis, which leads to procrastination and purposelessness.
- *Compromise*—Compromising values happens gradually over time—one little lie or indiscretion adds to another until, almost imperceptibly, integrity and character erode.
- *Hypocrisy*—Integrity is about actions matching beliefs.

A LIFE OF INTEGRITY

- If there is a lack of consistency between our public and private lives, then eventually we will be unable to manage the divide. Integrity will crumble.
- *Act boldly*—Bold acts issue from a person who has unshakable confidence. It is important to know the values and principles that drive your behavior.
- *Exhibit a great attitude*—The pursuit of integrity requires what is best and noble in your character.

- *Develop trust*—In the organizational setting in particular, trustworthiness is based on both character—what you are—and competence—how well you do what you do. It is "the foundation of trust."

CHANGE FROM THE INSIDE OUT

Let your yes be yes and your no be no.

Sincere, genuine, authentic, trustworthy. Are these words that are often heard when people describe you? Or how about *guarded, pretentious, closed, lacking character?* Without integrity and the trust it builds, you lose all ability to influence others. Leadership is all about influence.

- When someone asks you to do something, do you say, "I'll try," while silently wondering how you'll ever get to the project or maybe even knowing that you'll never be able to accomplish the task? What steps can you take to change in this area?
- In what areas of your life are you inconsistent?
- Do your values drive your behavior, or does political correctness take over? Explain.
- Do you believe that knowledge is power and therefore don't share everything you know? Or do you compartmentalize information and pass it out on a need-to-know basis? Or do you share information just to show people how much you know? How do these behaviors conflict with being a person of integrity?

13

Trusting One Another

To have a great organization, integrity must be widespread. It won't do to be a saintly leader of highest integrity if the rest of the team consists of liars, backbiters, and thieves. Integrity must exist from top to bottom.

As leader, you are the key. If you are a person of integrity, you will be trusted, and "trust has been shown to be the most significant predictor of individuals' satisfaction with their organization."[1]

Integrity and trust are inseparable; one cannot exist without the other. According to Charles O'Reilly and Karlene Roberts,

> Leaders who build trusting relationships within their team are willing to consider alternative viewpoints and to make use of other people's expertise and abilities. They feel comfortable with the group and are willing to let others exercise influence over group decisions. In contrast, managers in a distrustful environment often take a self-protective posture. They're directive and hold tight the reins of power. Those who work for such managers are likely to pass the distrust on by withholding and distorting information.[2]

In a research study several groups of business executives were asked to be involved in a role-playing exercise. The groups were given identical factual information about a difficult policy decision, and then they were asked to solve a problem related to that decision. Half of the groups were briefed to expect trusting behavior from the members of their group; the other half were told to expect untrusting behavior ("You cannot openly express feelings or differences with members of your group").

After thirty minutes of discussion, each group member as well as those who had observed the role playing completed a questionnaire. The responses were in harmony with each other: The discussions among members in the high-trust group were significantly more positive than the discussions among members of the low-trust group. In fact, people in the low-trust group who tried to be open and honest were virtually ignored. Hostility was caused by a mere suggestion, and it quickly spread throughout the group. The people in the low-trust groups realized that the lack of trust kept them from high achievement. They did not feel free to be vulnerable due to the actions and rejection of other group members.[3]

Here are some findings on the high-trust group:

- Members were more open about their feelings.
- Members experienced greater clarity of thinking.
- Members searched for more alternative courses of action.
- Members reported greater levels of mutual influence on outcomes.

The high-trust group opened the gate of personal vulnerability, and the result was a better team and a model of integrity-based leadership.

When people do not trust one another, it is difficult for the organization to succeed and for the people within the organization to feel completely fulfilled. People who feel trusted and who trust their leaders are more satisfied, and their work environment is less stressful. There exists a feeling of openness and confidence and a greater ability for people to believe they can take risks.

ORGANIZATIONAL INTEGRITY

How can you build a team of integrity? By modeling some key qualities.

Vulnerability

A leader who is approachable, available, and open to other ideas, thoughts, and even criticism has learned to be a humble person and further develops his or her integrity.

Executives often overlook the power of vulnerability. They confuse vulnerability with being weak. Too often, and for whatever reason (fear, circumstances, office politics, and so on), leaders build walls around themselves. They add one brick at a time until one day they become walled off from their people and their peers. The walls give them protection, but at the same time, the walls hide them from the harsh realities that confront every leader and keep them from communicating effectively. They are insulated and protected, but they are also cut off from others. Behind the walls, they can control and be hidden from failure. Behind the walls, they do not need to trust others or be vulnerable.

Gates, instead of walls, give others access to leaders, which enables leaders to demonstrate that they are trustworthy, open, and humble. Gates also allow leaders to share their visions and values with others. Open gates allow leaders to be vulnerable, to let go, and to trust others, which in turn builds *others'* trust in their leaders.

Abraham Lincoln made himself accessible to people as often as he could. He listened to them, cried with them, and found out about the war campaign from them. His habit of wandering around and listening to others offers an important management lesson. Donald Phillips writes,

> If subordinates, or people in general, know that they genuinely have
> easy access to their leader, they'll tend to view the leader in a more

positive, trustworthy light. "Hey," the followers think, "this guy really wants to hear from me—to know what I think and what's really going on. He *must* be committed to making things work!" And so Lincoln was.[4]

Once a leader takes this step of vulnerability, others will give back, and an effective team can be built on interpersonal integrity.

Ruth had been a leading medical expert in her company for many years. She had a reputation of being a hard-working, totally dedicated, innovative, top producer—but as an individual contributor. Then suddenly, just a couple of years before her retirement, Ruth found herself leading a team of people for the first time in her life. Ruth confided to me (Ron) that she realized her personal style worked fine for her as an individual but was totally unsuitable for leading people. She was concerned that her hard-driving, Type-A personality would be difficult for her team to deal with. And, in fact, when a feedback survey was conducted on her leadership style, Ruth received some critical remarks about her control of others and her domineering tendencies. She was very distraught. She wanted to leave the company with her good reputation intact but felt that this close to retirement she didn't have the time or the ability to change to a more effective style.

"I don't intend to be this way," she said. "That's just the way I am."

With some coaching, Ruth decided to share the survey results at her next team meeting and just be open and vulnerable. She revealed the data to her direct-reports in such a humble way that they completely rallied around her. As a team they worked out ways to ensure that Ruth's "demands" were met and yet also ensure that the team would be involved in the decisions. Ruth's last two years with the company were very rewarding.

Ruth has since retired, with a golden reputation, and her top two direct-reports were promoted to vice president.

Self-Disclosure

Leaders need to be the first to share what they stand for, what they value, what they want, what they hope for, and what they are willing to do in order to get where they want to go.

Self-disclosing leaders also need to be willing to risk trusting and being open with others if they want people's trust and openness in return. The only way to receive others' trust is to first trust others yourself.

Self-disclosure is risky for a leader. However, most people will appreciate the openness and will buy into a leader's plans, vision, dreams, and actions more easily than if a leader is walled off.

Prioritizing People-Development

In 1997 Dennis Brozak, the president of Design Basics, a company with revenues of $4 million, handed over day-to-day operations to Linda Reimer, a highly qualified fifty-three-year-old whom he had found three years earlier at, of all places, a copy machine. Brozak saw that Reimer had management potential, but the intensive systematic training he gave her was the key to her rapid advancement in the company.

> Back in 1991, Reimer was a longtime preschool director who wanted a part-time summer job. She took a low-level job photocopying blueprints for Design Basics, a company based in Omaha, Neb., that sells blueprints for homes via catalog. She did that job so well that Brozak hired her full-time in 1994.
>
> Over the next two years, Brozak gave Reimer various assignments that tested the potential executive's leadership capabilities. First, he made her a human resources director and asked her to switch the department's focus from advocating employees' rights to developing their professional growth. She succeeded. Brozak began challenging her more and more.

"I wanted to find out a lot about her," he says. "Can she manage and motivate people? Can she delegate accurately and appropriately? And she had to be able to fire people when necessary. She has a big heart, but she passed that test, too."

Then, to see if she understood the market and the industry, Brozak put Reimer in charge of one product, a catalog. The catalog's home designs sold well. Brozak then evaluated her financial acumen by making her an operations director, and he watched how well she used the company's money. Again, he says, she did well. So Brozak gave her control over all the company's publishing. Once more, she produced a hit.

Finally, Brozak tested Reimer, by then a vice president, with new product development. He figured that assignment would show whether she was a big-picture thinker. Reimer identified a new niche that has become a major profit center for the company. "She changed the direction of our sales," Brozak says.

By 1996, after 13 years at the company's helm, Brozak wanted more free time. He began passing day-to-day operations to Reimer, giving her new responsibilities gradually to make sure she was ready to be promoted. In April 1997, Reimer officially became president.[5]

If leaders want to develop others, they need to embrace these assumptions:
- "Everyone wants to feel worthwhile.
- Everyone needs and responds to encouragement.
- People buy into the leader before they buy into the plan.
- Most people don't know how to be successful.
- People are naturally motivated.
- Most people will move once they receive permission and equipping."[6]

Learning to Change

Another way a leader builds team integrity is through a willingness to make changes. How does a leader do that? How does a leader react when challenged or confronted by peers or subordinates?

Tom Peters is no stranger to change. He insists that embracing change is the single most competitive weapon in business. He suggests the following major points to help leaders effect change:

- "Trust/respect/don't underestimate potential.
- Insist upon (and promote) lifelong learning.
- Share information.
- Get customers involved.
- Emphasize 'small wins.'
- Tolerate failure to the point of cheerleading.
- Reject 'turf' distinctions."[7]

Trusting Others

When leaders work to create high-trust cultures within their organizations and to ensure a sense of security, people feel that they can trust one another.

Fostering employee loyalty is a tall order for a CEO. One old-fashioned gesture of trust is giving employees keys to the store. At Edson International in New Bedford, Mass., president Will Keene has given 7 of the 25 workers keys to the family-owned machine shop, which makes steering systems for yachts.

"These people have been with the company at least five years," says Keene. "They've made it known they plan to stay with our company for the long haul. They aren't out to rip us off." Newer employees get the message that long-term commitment is rewarded.

And the keys are used. Employees can work on their own projects in the shop on weekends, as long as someone else is present in case of injury. For workers who can't afford their own shop, it means a lot.[8]

Finding a Confidential Listener

What if you as a leader are working to build a high-trust organizational culture but still feel uncomfortable totally sharing your heart with others on your team or in the company? Find someone you can trust on the outside. You need someone who will mainly listen as you brainstorm ideas, let off steam, and regain perspective. By saying this we are not advocating that you stop being vulnerable or keeping gates open in your team or organization. But it is important for your health and well-being that you have someone, somewhere who can accept your total candor and maintain confidentiality. In some situations a consultant or a leadership coach performs this role.

THE INTEGRITY OF QUALITY

Many believe that quality and productivity will define the economics of the twenty-first century. One of the principal events of the last century was Japan's postwar emergence as an economic superpower. This came about primarily because of the quality revolution among Japanese manufacturers of automobiles and electronics, who zoomed past their American counterparts as consumers demonstrated with their wallets a preference for imports and the quality (perceived or real) of the products brought to the marketplace. In the process, American companies exported millions of jobs and, at the same time, were jolted into the reality that American consumers wanted, and even demanded, the highest quality.

To stop the outflow of consumer dollars, American manufacturers instituted many programs to improve quality. Total Quality Management (TQM) became more than just a popular catch phrase. It became a process driver for hundreds of companies and the focus of many leaders.

In 1985 Tom Peters and Nancy Austin wrote: "Any device to maintain quality can be of value. But all devices are valuable only if managers—at *all* levels—are living the quality message, paying attention to quality, spending time on it as evidenced by their calendars."[9]

The spotlight on quality remains. Today, consumers expect every product and service to be of the highest quality. Joseph Juran, publisher of the classic *Quality Control Handbook,* states, "We've made dependence on the quality of our technology a part of life."[10]

Clearly, American leaders need to emphasize quality in every aspect of their organizations. Whether they are service-driven or product-driven, company leaders must completely understand the need for quality and communicate that message down the line so that everyone in the organization fully understands the importance of maintaining and improving quality.

This addresses organizational quality, but what about *personal* TQM?

In the wake of the Enron and WorldCom scandals as well as other corporate meltdowns, investors have lost more than three hundred billion dollars and tens of thousands of people are out of work. Cooked books, deceitful executives, and lackadaisical board members have caused a collapse of inconceivable proportions. The disintegration of these companies represents an unimaginable failure of leadership and governance. What has happened to *personal* quality?

As you learn and apply the principles of trustworthy leadership presented in this book, you will become a leader known for personal "total quality." Specifically, no leader can have a life of quality without integrity. And the same is true for the entire organization. Without integrity, it will be impossible for the organization to have a truly high-quality reputation with customers, employees, peers, and shareholders.

Integrity is absolutely necessary for the success of a leader and an organization. A total quality life insists on integrity.

THE ESSENTIALS

- To have a great organization, integrity must be widespread.
- Integrity and trust are inseparable; one cannot exist without the other.
- When people do not trust one another, it is difficult for the organization to succeed and for the people within the organization to feel completely fulfilled.

ORGANIZATIONAL INTEGRITY

- *Vulnerability*—A leader who is approachable, available, and open to other ideas, thoughts, and even criticism has learned to be a humble person and further develops his or her integrity. Too often leaders build walls around themselves that keep them from trusting others or being vulnerable.
- *Self-disclosure*—Leaders need to be willing to risk trusting and being open with others if they want people's trust and openness in return.
- *Prioritizing people-development*—If leaders want to develop others, they need to embrace several assumptions. They need to recognize that everyone needs to feel worthwhile, that they need and respond to encouragement, that they must buy in to a leader before they will accept a plan, that they need to learn how to be successful, that they are naturally motivated, and that they need permission and equipping in order to act.
- *Learning to change*—Embracing change is the single most competitive weapon in business. Are you willing to change? How do you react when you are challenged or confronted?

- *Trusting others*—When leaders work to create high-trust cultures within their organizations and to ensure a sense of security, people feel that they can trust one another.
- *Finding a confidential listener*—Every leader needs a trusted confidant who will listen as the leader brainstorms ideas, lets off steam, and regains perspective.

THE INTEGRITY OF QUALITY

- Integrity is absolutely necessary for the success of a leader and an organization. A total quality life insists on integrity.

CHANGE FROM THE INSIDE OUT

Being vulnerable means giving out the keys to employees. It means being open to their ideas, suggestions, and criticism. The vulnerable leader opens gates instead of constructing walls.

- The following exercise may be helpful as you think about trust: Draw a circle and write the names of the people you wholeheartedly trust inside the circle. Pause a few moments after writing each name and ask yourself if you absolutely trust that person. There is nothing conditional about trust. Now, are there names you wish were inside the circle? What could you do that would result in greater trust? Next, what about the level of trust others have in you? How many people would put your name inside their trust circles? Are you satisfied with this number? What do you need to do to be more trusted by other people?
- What are the fears you face today? Take a few minutes and write down what you fear. It could be losing your job or missing the next big promotion. Whatever you list is real to you and keeps you from a total

quality life. Look at each fear on your list and try to discover what could help you overcome the fear. Do not fall into the blame game. You have this fear, and it is real to you. It is not someone else's responsibility or fault. It may make sense to take this list to a trusted friend. He or she may have some insight to help you work through your fear.

"Favored Are Those Who Calm the Waters"

A passionate man turns even good into evil and easily believes evil;
a good, peaceable man converts all things into good.

—THOMAS À KEMPIS, *The Imitation of Christ*

D oes it seem puzzling to find the term *peacemaker* included in a list of qualities necessary for a trusted leader? Does *peace* sound a bit too passive in today's business environment?

We are desperately in need of some peace and quiet. Work—all of life—is more stressful than ever before. James Citrin writes:

Late nights in the office. Early mornings to clear overnight e-mails. Weekends to catch up on all the things you didn't have time to do during the week. Most people in business simply cannot work harder or faster than they are at present—we're all sprinting just to keep up. As the old saw says, the race goes to the swift. And in the now-distant boom times, being first to market and hurrying obsessively to get out ahead made working in overdrive the norm.

But in our collective rush to get ahead, maybe we have lost something...certain actions, decisions, and initiatives do have their own rhythms, and we should be sensitive to them. Don't you agree that on some days, things just flow, while on other days, no matter how hard you push, things just don't move forward?[1]

A peacemaker is a leader who seeks to create calm within the storms of office politics, decision making, shareholder demands, cash-flow crunches, and the endless change of things the organization cannot control such as the economy, the weather, the fleeting loyalty of today's consumer, and a host of other constantly evolving issues.

One of the jobs of a leader is to prepare the organization for times of great demand. There have been many studies on the effects of overtime work. When additional hours of work are initially introduced, productivity climbs. However, research also shows that if the overtime continues for more than about two months, productivity falls back to its original level in spite of the additional hours worked. Leaders who neglect to give the organization rest will not be prepared when the real push comes. And, in fact, they are not getting a good return on their investment by keeping everyone working long hours over extended periods of time.

Leaders need to know when to let the organization (people) slow down and rest a bit so that they are ready to go when those two or three tough times during the year require that extra effort.

Take a look at your world. Some people on your team are fed up with the daily push and shove. They are overworked and worn out. They feel vulnerable and fearful, and they are seeking personal peace to do a job they feel they can do but for whatever reason cannot.

A good leader knows the value of bringing some calm to stressful situations. As Jesus once said to those under his leadership, "Peace I leave with you.... Do not let your hearts be troubled and do not be afraid."[2]

Peace means equilibrium, understanding, justice, mercy, caring, and harmony. To be a peacemaker means to quench the desire for revenge and replace it with the desire to put others first for their well-being.

However, peacemaking does not mean seeking peace at any cost, for the peacemaker realizes that peace at any price will usually result in events that are anything but peaceful. A peacemaker is not an appeaser. He or she is not a person who is easy to shove around and who refuses to take a position. We are not talking about wimpy leaders who avoid confrontation. Quite the contrary. A peacemaker understands the positive role of conflict in building a solid team. A peacemaker is one who through strength and knowledge establishes good relationships between estranged parties—relationships based on truth and fairness.

Peacemaking leaders encourage open discussion and honest debate, which actually improves relationships. Harmony comes from the trust that is developed, not from the suppression of discussion and debate. In fact, great peacemaking leaders create more energized debate than normal.

14

Calming Chaos

The world we live in is chaotic. A great leader learns how to leverage chaos into creativity, to bring a sense of tranquillity to a crazy world.

Dealing with new technology, profit expectations, continual new-product development, the fickle shopper, and global competitors requires perpetual change and lightning-fast reactions. Markets change, old competitors consolidate, new competitors emerge, and attempts at re-engineering threaten our daily bread. Both leaders and employees can soon feel under siege and at the mercy of chaos.

A creative, energy-filled *calm* is what we need. A word picture may aid our understanding of this. Imagine you are a surfer. There you are with your board, waiting for the "big one." If you are in Hawaii, the waves you are playing in might rise to twenty feet. All around you is surging, frothy chaos. Currents, tides, and the weather have combined to create a uniquely unstable environment. Conditions are always changing; every moment the ocean is different. If you try to catch a wave exactly the way you did yesterday, you will take a hard fall. You must stay alert and react quickly to every nuance of water, tide, and wind.

Gutsy leaders confront chaos. No one who is content to just paddle a surfboard beyond where the waves break has ever caught a "big one." Neither has such a person ever wiped out. If you want to ride a wave, you have to enter into the chaos. If you panic while riding a big wave, you are sure to wipe out. If you stay calm, you can have a wonderful ride while tons of water crash down around you.

Creating calm in the office requires a similar ability to assess the environment, to act quickly, and to stay calm. The economy, products, competitors, consumers, and employees all constantly change. Someone has to have answers; someone must be an independent thinker, able to calmly think things through.

We are familiar with a banker who had a client ready to sell a branch location of his business. The main location seemed to be prospering, but this particular branch appeared to be a drain on energy, time, and resources. The business owner was upset, but the banker remained calm. He took the time to analyze the underlying causes of the owner's problems. He visited the location, recast the numbers, and advised the owner *not* to sell the branch but to move and resurrect it. In reality, the branch location was producing extra cash, and the owner, following the banker's advice, turned his entire business around.

People will follow leaders who stay steady in the turbulence and work with them to create new answers, new plans, and a new future.

Whatever you do, don't slip into what we call the "arsonist's response to chaos."

The Fort Worth *Star-Telegram* reported that firefighters in Genoa, Texas, were accused of deliberately setting more than forty destructive fires. When caught, they stated, "We had nothing to do. We just wanted to get the red lights flashing and the bells clanging."

Do you know any leaders who intentionally start "fires" so they can get the "red lights flashing and hear the sirens"?

Leaders in one of our client organizations proudly described themselves as "firefighters." They were proud of the fact that they were good at hosing down crises. But when they were asked, "Is it possible you might also be arsonists?" it caused a great deal of reflection within the company.

The goal is a creative, steady productivity—not an out-of-control environment that squanders energy and resources on crisis management.

CREATIVITY OUT OF CHAOS

The irony is that a certain amount of chaos is necessary because "quality" chaos stimulates creativity. Organizations that do not create some space for creative chaos run the risk of experiencing staleness, loss, and even death.

"Life exists at the edge of chaos," writes Stuart Kauffman, author of *At Home in the Universe: The Search for the Laws of Self-Organization and Complexity*. "I suspect that the fate of all complex adapting systems in the biosphere—from single cells to economies—is to evolve to a natural state between order and chaos, a grand compromise between structure and surprise."[1]

If a leader fears the creative tension caused by chaos, trouble is often not far away. Leaders need to understand that creativity comes out of chaos, and even what has been created needs to be exposed to chaos just to make sure it is still viable and working. Even the new creation may need the chaos of re-creation to survive in a highly competitive world.

Meg Wheatley writes in her book *Leadership and the New Science,* "The things we fear most in organizations—fluctuations, disturbances, imbalances—are also the primary sources of creativity."[2] The question is, how do leaders get people from the scary, agonizing, and anxiety-filled feelings of chaos to the liberating place of creativity, change, and steadiness?

Before we answer that question, we do need to look at creativity and chaos. The reality of today's world is that millions of ideas for innovation, change, and improvement lie within any factory, distribution center, high-tech office, retail storefront, or operations center. You can also multiply that number by millions (or so it seems) when you bring people together in a team setting and allow them the freedom to create, innovate, and change. In many organizations this causes chaos and uncertainty.

Leaders, then, who understand the positive side of chaos can begin leading people through the confusing maze that creativity causes. They can help people understand that disruptions are opportunities. They can focus their attention on a building a culture that understands change and brings teams together, creating synergy among the members. These leaders explain how necessary it is for a company to respond to change in order to remain competitive.

Leaders help their employees understand the chaos going on around them by making meaning out of it. It is not easy, but it is so very necessary. "Leaders must have the ability to make something happen under circumstances of extreme uncertainty and urgency. In fact leadership is needed more during times of uncertainty than in times of stability: when confusion over ends and means abounds, leadership is essential."[3]

PEACE AND MAKING MEANING

How do leaders create peace in the midst of chaos? How do they restore an organization to the point of balance and productivity? How do leaders reach out to employees during times of uncertainty and worry?

By becoming peacemakers.

The major problem many leaders face is not the mechanics of change or even embedded resistance to change. The chief challenge is helping people understand what is going on around them. According to a national survey taken by the University of Michigan Institute for Social Research in the fall of 2001, only 1 in 5 adults said they felt hopeful about the future as compared with 7 out of 10 who reported feeling this way in a 1990 survey.[4] People are distressed and want someone to bring meaning to their daily lives.

Calm and team effectiveness come when a leader makes meaning out of the jumble of chaos that surrounds employees, suppliers, and consumers. In most situations, every person on a team brings a different point of view, a unique experience, or a personal preference to the table. Every market change brings with it new expectations, new competition, or new hopes. It also brings new opinions, new points of view, and new preferences. How does a leader make meaning out of all that?

Peacemakers focus outside themselves. Leaders who understand the need to make meaning for their teams and organizations understand that it starts with their own style. If we are self-centered and proud, we surrender the ability to see the angst in others. The prideful leader will not see the need for communication or helping others understand what is going on around them. Such leaders hold their cards close to the vest. Their focus is on themselves.

In contrast, leaders who put "you first" and have self-esteem based on humility are able to look beyond themselves and help others see meaning in their circumstances.

Peacemakers maximize opportunities for communication. We have a friend who says, "You need to tell people the story until you vomit—then tell them some more." Peacemakers take advantage of every opportunity to communicate with people to help them understand chaos and confusion. Communication is not just speaking; it involves listening, too. In true communication, a leader honors everyone's opinions and frames of reference. The goal is to learn, not necessarily to check items off the to-do list. This creates a "learning" organization or team that encourages and listens to everyone's opinions. Before making decisions, leaders of learning organizations probe the dissenters to better understand their opinions. They listen, learn, honor other people, and discover how to make great, lasting decisions.

Peacemakers encourage thinking. Even when people see change or confusion as an opportunity rather than a menace, they still need to feel safe and unafraid. Leaders need to create an environment that is open and flexible. Leaders need to encourage thinking that seeks the sustainability of improvements, not just the solutions to problems. In order for people to go that far, they need to feel supported and that their thoughts are being heard and acted upon.

Peacemakers understand the process of change. All too often we have seen that when chaos or change happens in an organization, leaders deal with the impact on a personal level but forget to bring the whole organization along with them. In her book *On Death and Dying*, Elisabeth Kübler-Ross explains that "all of our patients reacted to the bad news in almost identical ways, which is typical not only of the news of fatal illness but seems to be a human reaction to great and unexpected stress."[5] Her findings indicate that when humans are faced with difficult information, such as unavoidable change, we all go through the same pattern of denial, anger, depression, rationalization, and, finally, acceptance.

In business situations, we find a similar pattern at work:

1. *Denial*—This can't be happening to me/us.
2. *Anger*—Why is someone doing this to me/us?
3. *Depression or identity crisis*—What will I/we do in the new organization? Where is my/our place?
4. *Rationalization*—Yes it's true, but it doesn't apply to me/us for these reasons....
5. *Acceptance or the search for solutions*—How do I/we solve the problem?

While the members of a team deal with each stage a little differently and take varying amounts of time to reach acceptance, the team as a whole eventually gets through the process and is ready to search for and implement solutions. The problem is, leaders quickly forget or are not even aware of the fact that they first had to work their way through the other stages to get to this point. And so, equipped with the solution (or at least energized by the possibility of a solution), they announce to the organization with great fanfare how this new challenge will be tackled. But what kind of responses do they get from others in the organization? "Why are you doing this to us?" "Am I going to lose my job?" "How do I fit into this new organization?" "Your solution might be a good one, but you don't understand; it doesn't really apply to my part in the organization."

Leaders are often confused and angry when others don't seem to "get it" and eagerly jump on board with the plan. They assume that others are just not willing to deal with the change and be as open to the potential solutions as they themselves are. But, in fact, others may not be against the plan; they may just be working through the stages of understanding the issue or change. Leaders have simply forgotten that they went through these same stages.

The peacemaker who makes meaning out of chaos understands the change process and seeks to help others who are at different stages in the process understand the facts and feel comfortable in an evolving environment.

Peacemakers understand the longer-term view. Even as we stop focusing on ourselves, begin building interpersonal relationships, and seek to understand the progressive stages of change, we also need to take a longer-term view of the issues or changes. Too often people make small, short-term improvements that send their organizations into a rapid-fire series of chaotic adjustments; then they make more small changes that rip apart their employees' morale.

Peter G. Peterson, chairman of The Blackstone Group, said in an interview:

> Don't sacrifice your long-term vital future for the temporary present.
> Just as it is a mistake to assume that boom times go on forever (an
> assumption that got us into this e-commerce fiasco in the first place), it's
> also a mistake to assume that the business cycle has been repealed and
> that today's bad times will go on forever. The latter assumption can lead
> to so much emphasis on cutting costs today that we forget that we're
> also managers of the future.[6]

We are familiar with a company whose former president (and founder) took it through significant short-term changes only to reverse or change his decisions months or even weeks later. The result was a swelling of employee distrust and despair. The upshot of their negative attitude was the formation of an informal vigilante group within the company. The group simply began to ignore the changes or bury them so deeply within the bureaucracy that they were never enacted.

We use a concept called Beliefs and Assumptions to help organizations not only improve quality and interactions but also focus on longer-term solutions and thus avoid the needless pain and suffering that result from short-term chaos.

In the course of everyday business, work is performed and results are achieved. If the actual results do not match the desired results, we apply a fix and try again in an effort to achieve better results. However, this do-the-work-get-the-results-adjust-do-the-work cycle can become very repetitive and tiring. Thus, the TQM and re-engineering evolutions were born.

By examining the systems and processes that drive the work, we can make changes earlier in the cycle to avoid many of the undesirable results without getting caught in the trap of having to constantly fix problems. However, if leaders really want to make sustainable changes, they must examine the underlying beliefs and assumptions that form the basis for the systems and processes. Having a system or process in place is one thing. But the key to success is having people who believe in the process and the importance of implementing it.

When leaders focus on sustainability, they bring peace and a semblance of meaning to change. Rather than relying on knee-jerk responses, such leaders bring peace by looking farther down the road and developing solutions that have lasting power.

Many times leaders want to "fix" problems, so they just do some more work. They tinker with the system rather than providing a lasting solution.

Peacemakers seek long-term solutions. They want to improve the quality of thinking and interactions, not just fix problems. To do this, leaders who make meaning out of chaos work on beliefs and assumptions. They seek to get to the root of an issue and therefore develop a longer-term solution. They are also unwavering in this approach; anything less will cause confusion or chaos within the organization.

PLANT SEEDS OF PEACE

The times demand that leaders bring peace to their organizations and teams. They can do so by making meaning out of the mess. The times demand that flexibility and humility replace rigid systems and pride. The predictable environment is outdated, but to ensure quality, solid staff relationships, and employee achievement, leaders must embrace the peacemaker role and bring meaning to everything that is done or will be done.

This may sound like a daunting task. But even spreading a few small seeds of peace consistently will make such a difference—long term. One writer put it this way:

Take a seed the size of a freckle. Put it under several inches of dirt. Give it enough water, light, and fertilizer. And get ready. A mountain will be moved. It doesn't matter that the ground is a zillion times the weight of the seed. The seed will push it back.

Every spring, dreamers around the world plant tiny hopes in overturned soil. And every spring, their hopes press against impossible odds and blossom.

Never underestimate the power of a seed.

As far as I know, James, the epistle writer, wasn't a farmer. But he knew the power of a seed sown in fertile soil.

"Those who are peacemakers will plant seeds of peace and reap a harvest of goodness."[7]

Become a leader who sows seeds of peace.

THE ESSENTIALS

- A peacemaker is a leader who seeks to create calm within the storms of business.
- A peacemaker understands the positive role of conflict in building a solid team.
- Both leaders and employees can feel under siege and at the mercy of chaos. A creative, energy-filled *calm* is what we need.
- People will follow leaders who stay steady in the turbulence and work with them to create new answers, new plans, and a new future.

CREATIVITY OUT OF CHAOS

- "Quality" chaos stimulates creativity. Leaders who understand the positive side of chaos can begin leading people through the confusing maze that creativity causes.
- Leaders facilitate the understanding of chaos by making meaning out of what is going on around their people.

PEACE AND MAKING MEANING

- The chief challenge is helping people understand what is going on around them.
- *Focus outside ourselves*—If we are self-centered and proud, we surrender the ability to see the angst in others.
- *Maximize opportunities for communication*—In true communication, leaders honor everyone's opinions and frames of reference.

- *Encourage thinking*—Leaders need to create an environment that is open and flexible.
- *Understand the process of change*—The peacemaker who makes meaning out of chaos understands the change process and seeks to help others who are at different stages in the process understand the facts and feel comfortable in an evolving environment.
- *Understand the longer-term view*—Too often people make small, short-term improvements that send an organization into a rapid-fire series of chaotic adjustments. When leaders focus on sustainability, they bring peace and a semblance of meaning to change. Peacemakers seek long-term solutions.

PLANT SEEDS OF PEACE

- The times demand that leaders bring peace to their organizations and teams and that flexibility and humility replace rigid systems and pride.

CHANGE FROM THE INSIDE OUT

Stress is running rampant in our world today. We can't seem to get away from it; cell phones, wireless e-mails, and Wi-Fi (Wireless Fidelity) keep us connected all the time. People are experiencing more burnout than ever. We have found that productivity increases exponentially when people have some sense of control over their environment, when they understand the meaning of the changes and developments buffeting their lives. Today we may have more information and ability to stay connected; however, it is the leader who calms chaos who wins in the long term.

- How do you make sense and meaning of the events happening around you? What do you do to help others see the meaning of changes and events so they can make sense out of them?

- Would people describe you as a mature individual who seems to handle the setbacks and victories of life with calm and understanding? Are you a thermostat or thermometer? (Thermostats regulate the climate, while thermometers react to it.) Explain.
- When you are faced with an unsatisfactory result, do you just fix or tinker with the process, or do you really try to get to the beliefs and assumptions that are driving the behavior?

15

Dream Team

The Discovery Channel recently featured a program about a pride of fearsome lions. The documentary illustrated what happens when the leader is no longer able to preserve order and calm.

In one scene the lioness-leader of the pride is leading the hunt of a zebra. As she chases her prey, the frightened zebra jumps over a log at the very same time the lioness is trying to bring it down from behind. As they both leap, the zebra winds up violently kicking the lioness-leader in the head, inflicting a severe wound.

Over the next few weeks, the culture of the pride changes significantly. The lioness-leader becomes fearful and, because of the event with the zebra, shies away just at the moment of the kill. The pride gets visibly angry with her; they are hungry, and the lioness's traumatic experience has demolished the familiar, effective structure of the pride. She is no longer securing food. Her fear and tentative behavior have created chaos and caused a dysfunctional team that is confused and threatened by starvation.

During times of chaos and confusion, leaders can either be peacemakers, which will bring a calm that pulls the team together, or they can let a "kick to the head" at a decisive moment cause them to pull back, which will cause disruption, loss of morale, and uncertainty.

In our work with clients, most of the questions we receive concern how to find the key that opens the door to a successful team. Often the organization is in turmoil. It needs peace. It wants teamwork to lead the way out and beyond the current situation.

Peacemakers encourage teamwork. They seek group dynamics that unleash the right kind of power and the right attitude to achieve the best results.

How Can We Work Together?

Leaders at all levels grapple with the challenge of getting people to pool their talents and work with, not against, one another.

Often frustrating to leaders is a team that consists entirely of "stars" who can't or won't play together as a team to "win the championship." In an era of knowledge workers, leaders find themselves with nonfunctioning teams of all-stars who can easily undermine them. (Peter Drucker defines *knowledge workers* as those who "know more about their job than their boss does and in fact know more about their job than anybody else in the organization."[1])

Chuck Daly, the first coach of America's Dream Team, found himself needing to take basketball players like Michael Jordan, Magic Johnson, and Larry Bird and build a team of champions, not just a group of incredible superstars. Coach Daly used all his coaching experience, leadership ability, and basketball knowledge to mold this group of all-stars into a team.

The team dominated headlines as well as the competition. Everywhere they went, the media followed. And the animated, trash-talking practices were sometimes bigger news than the games. In their first Olympic game together, the Dream Team trounced Angola 116-48 and never looked back, going 8-0 en route to the gold.

They were the only undefeated team in the tournament, averaging an Olympic record of 117.3 points a game. They won their games by an average of 43.8 points, and the closest any opponent could come was 32 points (Croatia in the gold-medal final).

"You will see a team of professionals in the Olympics again," said Daly. "But I don't think you'll see another team quite like this. This was a majestic team."[2]

Coach Daly could not mold these incredibly talented basketball stars into the successful team they became by keeping the focus on himself. On the other hand, he could not surrender the basic basketball concepts he knew would help the *team* win a gold medal. He was a builder and a success at developing teams.

Teamwork doesn't just happen. A winning team is not formed by a miracle of nature. You cannot just throw people together (even knowledge workers or pro basketball stars) and expect them to function as a high-performance team. It takes work. And at the core of team building is the desire to develop people and create a calm environment in which productive growth and seasoning can occur.

When leaders tolerate poor teams or even promote them through their own leadership style, organizations find themselves misaligned. Employees use this out-of-plumb structure just like children who play off each quibbling parent to get their own way. Leaders need to stop this behavior and get teams realigned. Leaders sometimes empower direct-reports to perform tasks or projects that are actually opposed to each other.

When team members come to us, they also have questions. Typically the questions team members ask are about themselves: "How do I deal with difficult team members?" or "How do I get heard?" These are self-directed questions. The team members are concerned about themselves—getting heard, getting ahead, getting along, and getting their jobs done.

In most cases the leader has not developed the team to the point of understanding the full value of synergy. The team members do not understand that the sum of their collective output will be greater than the work they could do individually.

Worse, many executive teams are not convinced that synergy can happen at the leadership level. "Authors Robert Lefton and V. R. Buzzotta, long-time counselors to top management, systematically examined 26 top-level teams, ranging in size from six to 20 people (usually a CEO or president and vice presidents); 20 of the firms are in the Fortune 500 club. In a nutshell, the authors found little teamwork, virtually no 'synergy' from these collections of wise heads, and a lot of wasted time and childish behavior."[3]

It falls on leaders to get teams excited about working together—about creating synergy. Many of the team members' questions and wants can be overcome when they feel the power of working together and achieving the goals of the team.

BUILDING TEAM DYNAMICS

The basic question from leaders is therefore reduced to "How do I build teams without blowing the place up?" Following are some suggestions.

Start with the "Two Pillars"

This book is centered on eight principles of successful leadership. What we call the "two pillars"—the key principles that support and are intertwined with the others—are humility and endurance. A leader who desires to build a great team must first become a leader of humility and endurance. Pride and despair always force leaders to choose incorrect methods and solutions.

It is difficult to build a team when you need to be the center of attention, the only voice, the only one with an idea, and the only one who can make a decision. It is also difficult to build a team when, at every sour turn, the team stumbles and fails or doesn't learn from failure. Endurance means pushing through struggles together until the results are positive. Leaders, by the way they respond to crisis and chaos, often cause teams to quit sooner than necessary.

Michael Gershman, in his book *Getting It Right the Second Time*, squeezes forty-seven case studies into 256 pages. All teach one lesson: humility. And one credo: Try anything. Keep trying. Maybe you'll get it right someday. Endurance.[4]

The two pillars, humility and endurance, produce leaders who are ready to excite, energize, and develop teams.

Understand, Accept, and Communicate Change

Since the 1980s—or earlier—the business world has begun to see the need for entirely new models of management in order to succeed in regaining and defending competitiveness in today's world economy. The old paradigm of management that had guided the U.S. economy since the rise of the railroads and the large corporations of the Industrial Revolution no longer seemed to work. Firms struggled to remake themselves in order to be competitive. They followed the advice of many writers and consultants to become organizations that stepped away from Management by Objective and adopted a strategy of learning.

Today we live in a rapidly changing postindustrial society that is becoming increasingly complex and fluid. It is an environment that requires decision making and sometimes rapid change within organizations. Surviving and thriving in this rapidly changing landscape becomes a function of an organization's ability to learn, grow, and break down institutional structures within the organization that impede growth. Organizations that are ideologically committed to growth and change will be at an advantage in the postindustrial era.

In his book *Leading Change,* John Kotter explains how leaders can effectively communicate change in their organizations. All of us at one time or another fully understand the confusion caused by change. Kotter writes,

> Because the communication of vision [change] is often such a diffi-cult activity, it can easily turn into a screeching, one-way broadcast in which useful feedback is ignored and employees are inadvertently made to feel unimportant. In highly successful change efforts, this rarely happens, because communication always becomes a two-way endeavor.[5]

Even more important than two-way discussion are methods used to help people answer all the questions that occur during times of change and chaos. Clear, simple, often-repeated communication that comes from multiple sources and is inclusive of people's opinions and fears is extremely helpful and productive.

Manage Conflict

In his book *The Fellowship of the Ring,* the first book in the series The Lord of the Rings, J. R. R. Tolkien describes the camaraderie of a diverse group banded together by a common cause. Called "the fellowship of the ring," their quest is to destroy the power of the Dark Lord by destroying the ring in which that power resides. Though they differ in nearly every way—racially, physically, temperamentally—the fellowship is united in its opposition of the Dark Lord. In a section omitted in the movie, a heated conflict breaks out among the cru-saders. Axes are drawn. Bows are bent. Harsh words are spoken. Disaster nearly strikes the small band. When peace finally prevails, a wise counselor observes, "Indeed in nothing is the power of the Dark Lord more clearly shown than in the estrangement that divides all those who still oppose him."[6]

Conflict causes estrangement within teams, even the best teams. Therefore, managing conflict is at the heart of the dilemma of the leader who has good relations with individual team members but cannot get the group to work together.

Rivalry causes division. Debate causes hurt feelings or a sense of not being heard or understood. How does a leader keep an aggressive person and a person who easily withdraws engaged?

Kenneth W. Thomas and Ralph H. Kilmann created the Conflict Mode Instrument, which is "designed to assess an individual's behavior in conflict situations." It measures people's behavior along two basic dimensions: "(1) assertiveness—the extent to which an individual attempts to satisfy his or her concerns, and (2) cooperativeness—the extent to which an individual attempts to satisfy the other person's concerns. These two dimensions of behavior can be used to identify five specific methods of dealing with conflicts."[7] The methods are described as follows:

1. *Avoiding*—Low assertiveness and low cooperativeness. The goal is to delay.
2. *Competing*—High assertiveness and low cooperativeness. The goal is to win.
3. *Accommodating*—Low assertiveness and high cooperativeness. The goal is to yield.
4. *Compromising*—Moderate assertiveness and moderate cooperativeness. The goal is to find a middle ground.
5. *Collaborating*—High assertiveness and high cooperativeness. The goal is to find a win-win situation.[8]

Leaders need to use the peacemaking qualities defined by the two pillars of humility and endurance to bring conflict to the highest level of resolution: collaboration. The cooperative environment means "I need to be humble." The assertive environment means "I need to endure." The two pillars, taken together, cause people to listen, yet hold firm in solving conflict through collaboration. When collaborating, individuals seek to work with others to find a solution that satisfies all parties. It involves digging into hidden concerns, learning, and listening but not competing.

Treat Employees as Investors

It is interesting to watch privately held companies that seek to go public. They hire IPO (Initial Public Offerings) coaches who work hard with the CEO, CFO, and COO to train them to attract investors. They work with these leaders to help them say the right things in order to sell their companies. They teach them which messages work and which do not.

Our question: "Why don't companies do the same thing with employees?"

If you do a quick study on employee relations over the last several decades, we think you will discover that how employees are viewed and described has moved along a continuum from *workers* to *commodities* to *assets*. We do not believe that referring to employees as "assets" is a satisfactory description because so many leaders look at assets as disposable or upgradable. Leaders and companies would be more successful in building organizations if they thought of their employees as "investors."

Leaders need to give their people the same compelling we're-a-great-company-and-here's-why-and-where-we-are-going reasons for success that are promoted to IPO investors or current stockholders.

Leaders need to ask, "How can we get employees excited about what we are doing?" This approach is basic to team building and goes beyond vision and mission. It's a way to engage the greatest resource of people—their *energy!*

Alan Loy McGinnis, in his book *Bringing Out the Best in People,* tells us, "Talk may be cheap, but the right use of words can generate in your followers a commodity impossible to buy...hearts on fire."[9]

Isn't that what all leaders want—team members with hearts ablaze for the company's vision and goals? The leaders certainly want investors who are loyal, happy, and motivated to give resources. Treating your employees as investors will produce similar results.

CREATE A LEARNING ORGANIZATION

A learning organization differs from the MBO (Management by Objective) type of organizational structure in fundamental ways. In a learning organization individuals are continually reinterpreting their world and their relationship to it.

A learning organization incorporates the practice of continually challenging its paradigms and accepted ways of doing things. Built into the organization is a system that allows for the institutional structures and routine models of action to be regularly questioned and transformed.

As Peter Senge defines it, a learning organization is an organizational structure in which "people continually expand their capacity to create the results they truly desire, where new and expansive patterns of thinking are nurtured, where collective aspiration is set free, and where people are continually learning how to learn together."[10] In this sense, a learning organization is an organization that is continually expanding its ability to create and re-create the very patterns and structures by which it operates.

At least that is the goal.

Unfortunately, what we have found in our work is that quick decision making has won. In many cases, leaders have abandoned the learning organization in favor of the quick-deciding organization.

In times of chaos, confusion, and change, peacemaking leaders need to focus attention on making sure their organizations are quick learning rather than quick deciding.

The fast-paced environment of product development, competition, and shareholder expectations has forced many organizations to adopt a quick-deciding mentality. In this model, a team (much like a football team needing to score before time expires in the fourth quarter) is in a hurry-up offense. The goal is to make decisions. But as Tom Peters correctly observes, "As competition around the world boils over as never before, firms caught with bloated staffs and dissipating strengths—from Silicon Valley to the Ruhr Valley in Germany—are looking for quick fixes. There are none."[11]

So how would a two-pillar, peacemaking leader respond?

The goal of the quick-learning team is to seek out and develop opinion rather than steamrolling over it or quickly mustering forces against it. Feedback is highly desired rather than feared.

In contrast, feedback is offensive when you are a quick-deciding team. You develop "sides" on all issues. The competition heats up. Winning at all costs is what counts.

Members of a quick-learning team are all on the same side of the fence, looking at an issue with differing opinions, experiences, and ideas.

Meeting agendas are often a surprising enemy. Leaders, staring at an agenda, feel compelled to make decisions within the time allotted. In most cases, true discussion of the issues and everyone's opinions (the rooting-out process) is bypassed in favor of table talk that centers on implementation.

We suggest a meeting agenda that maps out what the team wants to learn about an issue. Learning should be the goal with good decisions the result. Remember that the goal is learning quickly and then making good decisions, not just deciding quickly.

"Patience," said Saint Augustine, "is the companion of wisdom." Problems and day-to-day crises test our wisdom and our ability to make decisions under pressure. Great leaders are people of patience and constant learning.

It is the leader's job to pull everything together into a quick-learning rather than a quick-deciding environment. The leader holds the dialogue together and asks questions that are designed to help team members clearly communicate their information and thoughts about the agenda item. In this way, the meeting's goal is met: quick learning—rather than quick deciding—for the purpose of making good decisions.

The leader needs to develop not only an inclusive mind-set but also one that honors people for who they are and what they bring to the process. Each person brings unique strengths and outlooks to the table.

So many books, articles, and seminars are developed to help leaders understand how to build teams. It's ironic that on a moment's notice during a terrible crisis several people facing impossible odds came together and built a successful team.

In what the news headlines called "The Miracle at Quecreek," nine miners, trapped for three days 240 feet underground in a water-filled mine shaft, "decided early on they were either going to live or die as a group."

The fifty-five-degree water threatened to kill them slowly by hypothermia, so according to one news report, "When one would get cold, the other eight would huddle around the person and warm that person, and when another person got cold, the favor was returned."

"Everybody had strong moments," miner Harry B. Mayhugh told reporters after being released from Somerset Hospital in Somerset, Pennsylvania. "But any certain time maybe one guy got down, and then the rest pulled together. And then that guy would get back up, and maybe someone else would feel a little weaker, but it was a team effort. That's the only way it could have been."

They faced incredibly hostile conditions together, and they all came out alive together.[12]

We think the Quecreek story pretty well illustrates ideal team dynamics. Being a contributor on an effective team and working together to accomplish a meaningful mission is a deep desire of many. It's up to the peacemaking leader to coach that team…of so many dreams.

THE ESSENTIALS

- Peacemakers encourage teamwork.

How Can We Work Together?

- A winning team is not formed by a miracle of nature. And at the core of team building is the desire to develop people and create a calm environment in which productive growth and seasoning can occur.
- It falls on leaders to get teams excited about working together—about creating synergy.

Building Team Dynamics

- *Start with the "two pillars"*—A leader who desires to build a great team must first become a leader of humility and endurance.
- *Understand, accept, and communicate change*—Surviving and thriving in this rapidly changing landscape becomes a function of an organization's ability to learn, grow, and break down institutional structures within the organization that impede growth.
- *Manage conflict*—Conflict causes estrangement within teams, even the best teams. Leaders need to use the peacemaking qualities defined by the two pillars of humility and endurance to bring conflict to the highest level of resolution: collaboration.
- *Treat employees as investors*—Leaders and companies would be more successful in building organizations if they thought of employees as "investors."

CREATE A LEARNING ORGANIZATION

- A learning organization incorporates the practice of continually challenging its paradigms and accepted ways of doing things.
- In many cases, leaders have abandoned the learning organization in favor of the quick-deciding organization.
- Members of a quick-learning team are all on the same side of the fence, looking at an issue with differing opinions, experiences, and ideas.
- Learning should be the goal with good decisions the result.
- The leader needs to develop not only an inclusive mind-set but also one that honors people for who they are and what they bring to the process.

CHANGE FROM THE INSIDE OUT

Nothing breaks down the cohesiveness of an organization more than friction and divisiveness within a leadership team.

Factors that are closely linked with financial performance are good integration and coordination of teams throughout an organization. By not building strong team bonds, you are bypassing one of the best finance-generating aspects of corporate culture.

As a former civil engineer, I (Ron) am familiar with how concrete blocks stand up to pressure. At some point when the pressure gets to be too great, the concrete block crumbles into small pieces. It granulizes. But if you reinforce that concrete by crisscrossing it with reinforcing rods, it can handle much higher pressures and remain intact. Team building adds the reinforcing rod to teams. Friction and divisiveness serve only to granulize them.

- Do you believe that competition on your team is good? Will it let the cream rise to the top? Explain.

- How does helping your team develop a collaborative approach to incorporate their strong drives and opinions bring out the best in all the team members?
- When you develop teams, one place to start the process is to think and talk in terms of *our* goals. It is not about *your* goals; it is about the shared goals of the team. One exercise may be to audit your language. "Take a piece of paper and divide it into two columns. Write *we* at the top of one column and *I* at the top of the other. Ask someone to listen to one of your speeches or meetings and count the number of times you say *I* and the number of times you say *we*.... Those who use *I* more than *we* will make poor leaders, and the organizations will suffer from their attempts to claim credit for themselves"[13] rather than building teams.

Standing Strong

On October 29, 1941, as the world reeled from the onslaught of the Nazi regime in Europe and faced a looming threat from Japan, Winston Churchill was asked to speak at Harrow, his old school. Near the end of his two-page speech, Churchill spoke the now famous words: "Never give in, never give in, never, never, never—in nothing, great or small, large or petty—never give in except to convictions of honour and good sense."

Churchill had experienced many crushing setbacks throughout his life and political career, yet he refused to give up. He was a man of extreme courage and endurance.

When leaders make decisions, seek to expand an organization's borders, or want to execute an innovative idea or create change, they will encounter opposition and face the great temptation to conform or quit. How can they resist and stand strong? How can they acquire the bulldog will of a Winston Churchill and never give up?

Endurance is the result of two foundational character qualities: courage and perseverance. Both are required of leaders seeking the trust of others.

No Guts, No Glory

"Holding the hill" when under fire can be a terrifying and lonely experience. A leader will face a long list of challenges, which, if not faced and disarmed, can turn the most competent person into a faltering coward. We have grouped these pitfalls to courage into two categories: doubt and avoidance.

Defeating Doubt

This foe of courageous leadership comes in a variety of flavors.

First, there are the *personal doubts*. We may doubt our abilities, our judgment, our talents, and even our faith. We look at a problem and cannot find a solution. We attempt to fix it but cannot. Doubt oozes into our minds, and we are frozen into inactivity.

Then there are the *doubts about our teams* or others we depend upon. Have you ever worked with people who are overwhelmed, stressed out, resistant to change, burned out, not working together, complainers, rumor spreaders, backstabbers, noncommunicators, whiners, stubborn hardheads, blamers, or unmotivated negative thinkers? When encountering such bad attitudes and behaviors that stall the progress of our teams, we are tempted to slide into despair, and our backbones turn to mush.

Next is *doubt in the organization*. We may see the company sliding down a hill to mediocre performance, abandoning the right values and a vibrant vision. It's one thing to maintain your own personal courage in the place where you have influence. But it's overwhelming to stand strong when the larger organization is waffling on its mission and embracing plans that seem doomed in the face of aggressive market competition. Your knees start to knock.

Also doubts may surface when *organizational outsiders,* like stockholders, start questioning our forecasts and plans. A real-life example of such an incident took place in 2000 when shareholders of CDNow, an online retailer of CDs and videos, filed a lawsuit claiming that the company had misled them "by delaying the disclosure of a negative report from the company's auditors that questioned CDNow's viability."[1] The suit charged that withholding this information from shareholders constituted a violation of federal securities laws.

Following this incident, CDNow was acquired by another media conglomerate. The company is still in business, but just imagine the meetings, plan changes, and despair that occurred during this stressful incident.

To endure as a leader, you will have to disarm doubt with gritty courage.

Arresting Avoidance

M. Scott Peck wrote that the "tendency to avoid problems and the emotional suffering inherent in them is the primary basis of all human mental illness."[2]

Another courage-crippler is refusing to confront reality and act. If we employ avoidance tactics when we are tested and struggle, we will end up with even more frustration and trouble. We have seen organizations take giant steps to avoid any kind of pain and suffering. But the result is a dysfunctional organization, not a great company.

To quote Winston Churchill again, "One ought never to turn one's back on a threatened danger.... If you meet it promptly and without flinching, you will reduce the danger by half."[3] Avoidance confuses the entire organization. It causes "mental illness" in the company and on your team.

Avoidance-oriented people tend to move away from things that threaten them in order to protect themselves. Why? There are a number of reasons. Often it is due to excessive concern about *embarrassment*. We just don't want to be embarrassed or, more often, to embarrass someone else. We hold back—we don't tell the truth—and poor organizational or personal behaviors are perpetuated.

Fear is another culprit. Sometimes it just seems easier to run and hide. Maybe the issue will somehow just go away? That's classic avoidance—a sign of cowardly leadership.

In the movie *Panic Room,* Jodie Foster plays a woman who is frightened by burglars who have broken into her New York City condominium. She retreats with her daughter to a high-tech panic room that is actually part of her residence.

According to ABC News, panic rooms are not just in the movies. Security companies regularly install what they refer to as "safe rooms." Most requests come from wealthy families or celebrities who fear being targets of kidnappers, stalkers, or home invaders. It is estimated that there are thousands of such rooms in Bel Air and Holmby Hills in Southern California.[4]

How many leaders seek the safety of their own panic rooms?

Another reason for avoiding problems can be *oversensitivity* to the feelings or opinions of others. We just don't want to hurt anybody. The other person is so nice; why should she have her parade rained upon? Issues are circumvented, and facts are ignored. We avoid the short-term pain and inflict a longer-term problem within the team and the organization.

And then there is the old standby character quality that causes so many problems: unhealthy *pride*. Some of the people who are most adept at avoidance are very proud, especially if exploring the gory details of an organizational issue might make them look bad.

Leaders who develop a humble heart and a willingness to confront concerns do not allow pride to interfere. They are open to opportunities for self-growth because they are secure in who they are and are not preoccupied with themselves.

Avoidance holds back an organization whereas a commitment to improvement will positively influence your own development as well as the development of interpersonal relationships, teams, and overall company effectiveness.

It takes great courage to change a pattern of avoidance and seek instead to make improvements and overcome the pain or difficulty in making decisions, confronting people, or being overwhelmed by circumstances or self-doubt. It is not easy, but the benefits you will experience from making this change are far greater than the "benefits" of avoidance.

Freedom from avoidance enables leaders to focus attention on determining when a situation needs action and improvement. Personally, we rely on God's direction and do not take all the pressure ourselves. Many times the Bible provides the direction we need to finish the course and encourages us to set aside doubt and avoidance and develop true courage.

HOLDING STRONG

For two years scientists sequestered themselves in an artificial environment called Biosphere 2. Inside their self-sustaining community, the Biospherians created a number of mini-environments, including a desert, a rain forest, even an ocean. Nearly every weather condition could be simulated except one, wind.

Over time the effects of their windless environment became apparent. A number of acacia trees bent over and even snapped. Without the stress of wind to strengthen the wood, the trunks grew weak and could not hold up their own weight.

Holding strong and enduring as a leader requires some "wind." Adversity gives leaders an opportunity to strengthen themselves, discover what they believe, and communicate their vision and values to other people. There will be difficult times, but the difficult times—the windy days—help leaders grow stronger in their roles and in their faith and trust.

Holding strong comes with the turf. If you are standing strong for values and vision and for being a better leader, you will experience persecution and times of discouragement, adversity, and frustration.

Holding strong is a process. This is when a mentor can be so helpful by coming alongside the leader and objectively pointing out ways and opportunities to hold strong over an extended period of time.

Holding strong is also a journey. Doing the right thing can be stressful, complicated, and time-consuming, but ultimately, it brings fulfillment. Leaders need to focus on the small victories gained along the way. The journey builds character and confidence. The journey is rewarded when a leader sees the growth of his or her people, the growth of the business, and the achievement of the task.

After a career working at several jobs (railroad fireman, insurance salesman, Ohio River steamboat operator, and tire salesman), a forty-year-old man began cooking for hungry travelers who came by his service station in Corbin, Kentucky. He didn't have a restaurant, so he served his eager customers on his own dining table in the adjoining living quarters.

It wasn't long before more and more people came by to sample his food, so he moved his business across the street to a motel and restaurant. There he spent nine years serving customers and perfecting his special recipe for fried chicken.

In the 1950s "progress" caused the new highway to run around Corbin, and the man's business ended. By this time he had retired and was living on his monthly $105 Social Security check. He began going from restaurant to restaurant, cooking his famous chicken. If the owners liked the recipe, a handshake agreement gave the restaurant the recipe in exchange for a nickel for every chicken dinner sold.

By 1964 this little endeavor had become a sizable business. The man, Colonel Harland Sanders, had licensed over six hundred franchises to cook his tasty chicken recipe.[5] Ready to retire again, he sold his interest for two million dollars and became a spokesperson for the company. "In 1976, an independent survey ranked the Colonel as the world's second most recognizable celebrity."[6]

Colonel Sanders did not allow himself to be defeated. He held strong and was not overcome by discouragement. How can we develop a similar attitude toward adversity?

ADVERSITY AND DISCOURAGEMENT

"A man stopped to watch a Little League baseball game. He asked one of the youngsters what the score was. 'We're losing 18-0' was the answer.

'Well,' said the man. 'I must say you don't look discouraged.'

'Discouraged?' the boy said, puzzled. 'Why should we be discouraged? We haven't come to bat yet.'"[7]

Discouraged? Hardly. The boy was holding strong to the hope that his team could overcome any deficit. He was holding strong to his convictions.

No matter what the source may be, discouragement and adversity have a purpose:

- to deal with our pride
- to get our attention
- to get us to change our behavior
- to prepare us for future service

There are some wrong responses to adversity and discouragement, and they cause bitterness, doubt, depression, and hopelessness. But holding strong produces some right responses:

- We gain our team's trust because our actions match our intentions.
- We focus on seeing things through rather than abandoning our values or vision.
- We rely on God for the ability to endure.

We want you to build courage and persevere, to realize the sweet taste of standing strong for the long haul. *Endurance.*

They're not especially gifted.
They're just in it for the long haul,
that's all.
Heroes don't quit.
They are marathon runners
who won't walk away
from what they agreed to do.
They complete what they start,
though their feet may stumble.

When they fall, they are humble enough
to brush themselves off
and bury their pride
and regain their stride once again.
Heroes pace themselves by facing the fact
that they come from a long line of finishers
who cheer them on
from the bleachers of eternity.[8]

THE ESSENTIALS

- Endurance takes courage—guts. It takes the ability to persevere and hold strong when the tide of public opinion and employee wishes are against whatever you as leader believe must happen.
- When leaders make decisions, seek to expand an organization's borders, or want to execute an innovative idea or create change, they will encounter opposition and face the great temptation to conform or quit.

No Guts, No Glory

- *Defeating doubt*—We may doubt our abilities, our judgment, our talents, and even our faith. There are personal doubts, team doubts, organizational doubts, and doubts from outsiders. To endure as a leader, you will have to disarm doubt with gritty courage.
- *Arresting avoidance*—Embarrassment, fear, oversensitivity, and pride move leaders to avoid rather than confront problems. Avoidance holds back an organization whereas a commitment to improvement will positively influ-

ence your own development as well as the development of interpersonal relationships, teams, and overall company effectiveness.

HOLDING STRONG

- Adversity gives leaders an opportunity to strengthen themselves, discover what they believe, and communicate their vision and values to other people.
- Holding strong comes with the turf of being a great leader; it is a process, a journey that takes time.

ADVERSITY AND DISCOURAGEMENT

- No matter what the source may be, discouragement and adversity have a purpose: to deal with our pride, to get our attention, to get us to change our behavior, and to prepare us for the future.

CHANGE FROM THE INSIDE OUT

Dogged endurance is an important quality, but if it is directed down the wrong path, it can damage people, teams, and organizations. To endure, a leader must build on a foundation of humility, trust, compassion, commitment, focus, and integrity. Without holding firm to the other seven attributes on your way to endurance, you can never be assured that you are staying on the true and right path.

- Have you developed a leadership style (one that includes humility, trust, compassion, and integrity of a Trust-Me leader) that has equipped you to endure? If not, where has the process broken down for you? What steps do you need to take to change your style?

- On what are your personal values based? Are they based on greed and "me-first" concepts that get pushed at you every day, or are they based on something greater (the greater good of another human being, the greater good of the company, the greater good of humanity)?

The Enduring Organization

A phrase that to this day reminds Americans of selfless courage and heroic sacrifice is "Remember the Alamo."

The early history of the Alamo did not signal that someday it would become a shrine of freedom. Originally named Misión San Antonio de Valero, the Alamo was used by missionaries for decades before the Spanish seized the site for nonreligious purposes in 1793.

The Alamo thereafter housed a changing guard of military units representing Spanish, Mexican, and rebel forces until December 1835 when Ben Milam led a group of Texan and Tejano volunteers in a siege against Mexican-occupied San Antonio. After several days of intense street fighting, Milam's warriors drove the Mexicans from the city, and the Texans staked claim to and fortified the Alamo.

The Mexican General Santa Anna decided to teach the upstart rebels—and all Texans—a lesson. On about February 23, 1836, a contingent of thousands from Santa Anna's army invaded San Antonio, and the battle was on. When the first shots were fired, only about 150 Texans were at the Alamo to mount a defense under the joint command of William B. Travis and Jim Bowie. The day after the battle began, Colonel Travis said: "I am determined to sustain myself as long as possible and die like a soldier who never forgets what is due to his own honor and that of his country—*victory or death.*"[1]

Santa Anna's troops battered the Alamo mercilessly. Travis and Bowie slipped couriers through enemy lines to go plead with residents of nearby communities to send reinforcements to defend San Antonio. On the eighth day of the siege, a small group of thirty-two volunteers from Gonzales finally arrived, bringing the number of defenders to about two hundred.[2] The battle raged for another five days. As the likelihood of defeat increased, Travis gathered the men and drew a line in the dirt, asking the men willing to stay and fight to the death to step over. All but one did. Among those who stayed was the famous frontiersman David Crockett.

"The final assault came before daybreak on the morning of March 6, as columns of Mexican soldiers emerged from the predawn darkness and headed for the Alamo's walls. Cannon and small arms fire from inside the Alamo beat back several attacks. Regrouping, the Mexicans scaled the walls and rushed into the compound. Once inside, they turned captured cannon on the Long Barrack and church, blasting open the barricaded doors. The desperate struggle continued until the defenders were overwhelmed."[3]

None of the 189 soldiers defending the Alamo lived. The Mexican attackers lost an estimated sixteen hundred men.[4] The Texans may have lost the battle at the Alamo, but their sacrifice so enraged and energized others in the territory that just six weeks later the Mexicans were defeated for good at San Jacinto. The rallying cry in that great victory was "Remember the Alamo."

Colonel Travis was a leader who understood that perseverance for "the cause" is essential. Personal values translate into organizational values, and it takes persistence to communicate those values to everyone in the organization. Every day there are reasons to stray from deep personal values, but great leaders do not easily give them up or modify them in the face of pressure.

This kind of perseverance comes from a deep sense of purpose for life and from trusting in something outside ourselves. Personally, we believe it involves looking beyond ourselves and seeking to trust God for the answers, the vision, and the hope to persevere.

Persistence is also important as organizations and leaders create new products and strategies or make decisions. Some organizations do not stick with something long enough to actually make it happen. They create a company full of orphaned projects, ideas, goals, and mandates.

This is particularly a symptom of the quick-deciding company we discussed earlier. The quick-deciding company or team moves rapidly from decision to decision. Rather than taking time to learn from others, seek input, or teach in order to find quality, long-term solutions, the goal is deciding in a hurry. An organization's goal needs to be quick learning so that good decisions can be made as soon as possible.

If you have experienced some success with the previous seven principles, you are now ready to build an enduring organization.

BUILDING AN ENDURING ORGANIZATION

It is important for leaders to ensure that their direct-reports become great leaders too. Many leaders enjoy serving under leaders whose style is balanced by humility and endurance, but when leading their own teams, they adopt an autocratic leadership style. In most cases they do this because they do not think the people under them are as good as they are in their respective jobs (prideful thinking). They say to themselves, "I can handle the style of *my* leader, but my people can't function to the level we need them to under that style, so I'll be more controlling and autocratic." These leaders lack the perseverance to build leadership depth within the organization.

An example of the right kind of enduring development can be found in General Electric's Crotonville facility—America's first Corporate University and a symbol of GE's commitment to training within the organization. Jack Welsh and subsequent key leaders were there teaching, helping, encouraging, and building future leaders. They showed, by their example and hands-on approach, that building leaders was an integral part of General Electric's sustained success.

Do you remember Newton's Cradle? That finely built desk toy sat on many desks in many offices around the country. It was usually made of some beautiful cherry wood with polished steel balls hung from nylon strings, all hanging in a nice row between the ends of the cradle. Each steel ball was tightly secured to the top, but if a person pulled one or two of them and let them go, they would bang continuously against the other balls.

We have been working with two CEOs over the last few years whose leadership styles have so many similarities that we decided to give the style a name: the Newton's Cradle approach to leadership. These two leaders developed a very tight and trusting relationship with each member of their teams. Everyone talked of them as "great" leaders and the kind of bosses for whom employees would do anything. However, these two leaders would send one or more of their direct-reports off on a mission that was bound to conflict with a similar mission of another direct-report. The leaders, however, would never make any effort to help the direct-reports reconcile the conflicts. They would just let them bang against one another until one was victorious—Newton's Cradle.

For example, they would tell their CFO or COO that they must do whatever it took to control costs for the next quarter or two while, at the same time, encouraging the CIO to move ahead and implement the great, new, and costly computer system. This creates tremendous tension and turmoil throughout an organization as each person, feeling empowered by his or her boss, either joins the battle with the other direct-report or completely ignores him or her in dogged pursuit of individual goals.

Unfortunately, the Newton's Cradle leader does not see the value of bringing every part of the organization together into a highly functional, persevering team.

In their book *The Leadership Engine,* Noel Tichy and Eli Cohen write that the best companies have "good leaders who nurture the development of other leaders at all levels of the organization." Instead of defining reality for their workers, these leaders urge their workers to see reality themselves and mobilize the appropriate responses. Tichy and Cohen go on to discuss how much time many chief executives spend "formally and informally" on teaching. They conclude that the success of those firms is a direct result of everyone's pulling in the same direction. "All of the winning leaders I've studied share a passion for people. They draw their energy from helping others get excited about improving their business. And they energize their people at every opportunity with stimulating ideas and values."[5]

The kind of leadership Tichy and Cohen write about is one that encourages leaders to develop other leaders. It is a primary focus for the leader who wants to build an enduring organization.

THE MATURITY TO PERSEVERE

A quote from the Bible says, "Whenever trouble comes your way, let it be an opportunity for joy. For when your faith is tested, your endurance has a chance to grow. So let it grow, for when your endurance is fully developed, you will be strong in character and ready for anything."[6]

When leaders develop endurance or perseverance, they also develop maturity—not only within themselves but also within their organizations and teams. Perseverance breeds character as we stick to the task, bring others along with us, and develop an enduring organization. According to Julien Phillips and Allan Kennedy,

> Success in instilling values appears to have had little to do with charismatic personality. Rather it derives from obvious, sincere, sustained personal commitment to the values the leaders sought to implant, coupled with extraordinary persistence in reinforcing those values.[7]

Persevering leaders understand the importance of bringing every part of the organization along with them. It is a time-consuming and focused activity that will eventually yield tremendous results in overall morale, productivity, and team/employee support.

A leader needs to understand that he or she may quite naturally have an easy time focusing on the future or on how the future will look when certain projects, tasks, or goals are completed. Others within their teams may not be able to clearly or easily see the future, or they may be naturally pessimistic about anything involving the future. A leader needs the persistence to bring these people along—they are valuable to the team's overall balance. They may simply need the leader to either ask them questions to propel them into the future or help them visualize steps to the future outcome.

Bringing an organization along also involves being particularly effective during times of change. Many on the team will naturally resist change, so leaders need to humbly and calmly coax people along to the new direction or vision.

The story is told that Andrew Jackson's boyhood friends just couldn't understand how he became a famous general and then the President of the United States. They knew other men who had greater talent but never succeeded.

One of Jackson's friends said, "Why, Jim Brown, who lived right down the pike from Jackson, was not only smarter but he could throw Andy three times out of four in a wrestling match. But look where Andy is now."

Another friend responded, "How did there happen to be a fourth time? Didn't they usually say three times and out?"

"Sure, they were supposed to, but not Andy. He would never admit he was beat—he would never stay 'throwed.' Jim Brown would get tired, and on the fourth try Andrew Jackson would throw him and be the winner."

Picking up on that idea, someone has said, "The thing that counts is not how many times you are 'throwed,' but whether you are willing to stay 'throwed.' " We may face setbacks, but we must take courage and go forward in faith.... The battle is the Lord's, so there is no excuse for us to stay "throwed!"[8]

A. B. Meldrum once said, "Bear in mind, if you are going to amount to anything, that your success does not depend upon the brilliancy and the impetuosity with which you take hold, but upon the ever lasting and sanctified bull-doggedness with which you hang on after you have taken hold."[9]

Most of my (Ron's) clients would probably never hire me if I told them it was going to take five years to complete the major changes we talk about at the beginning of many of my consulting assignments. At one high-tech company, after three years of intensive effort to develop a new leadership style and corporate culture, the leadership team asked me to evaluate how they were doing. I asked them to rank their "completeness" in each of several major change categories. Overall, they ranked themselves at about 60 percent. I admitted that if they had asked me at the beginning of the process how long it was going to take, I would have estimated five years—so 60 percent after three years was just about right.

One strong leader whom I'm working with now took over an assignment three years ago in one of America's largest corporations. When he was hired he was actually identified as the "change agent" that the company needed. Needed, maybe, but certainly not wanted. After three years of struggling with the internal practices of the company, he has finally assembled a leadership team that should be able to carry out the many changes that are needed to meet the firm's looming challenges. I can recall many one-on-one conversations with him over the last three years when he wondered if he had the energy to keep going and whether it would be worth it in the end. But he has endured. I believe he will pick the fruit of an enduring company.

Throughout the history of man, the greatest achievements have been accomplished by leaders having an against-all-odds tenacity. The unshakable convictions of the rightness of their causes have kept adventurers, explorers, entrepreneurs, and visionaries going despite overwhelming difficulty and fierce competition. They were and continue to be persistent, holding fast to their beliefs and moving the idea or the organization forward.

That's the path to building an enduring organization.

THE ESSENTIALS

- Personal values translate into organizational values, and it takes persistence to communicate those values to everyone in an organization.
- Perseverance comes from a deep sense of purpose for life and from trusting something outside ourselves.

Building an Enduring Organization

- It is important for leaders to ensure that their direct-reports become great leaders too.
- Unfortunately, the Newton's Cradle leader does not see the value of bringing every part of the organization together into a highly functional, persevering team.

The Maturity to Persevere

- When leaders develop endurance or perseverance, they also develop maturity—not only within themselves but also within their organizations and teams.

- Persevering leaders understand the importance of bringing every part of the organization along with them.
- Bringing an organization along involves being particularly effective during times of change.
- Leaders "face setbacks" but must "take courage and go forward in faith."
- Great leaders continue to be persistent, holding fast to their beliefs and moving the idea or the organization forward.

CHANGE FROM THE INSIDE OUT

Picture Newton's Cradle, those steel balls banging against each other. Is that the kind of leadership style and organization you want to create? Or do you want to create something more enduring—something that will last? a legacy to your leadership?

Building that enduring organization requires developing attributes that last—that taproot, the cornerstone. The concepts described in this book have survived over two thousand years of turmoil, change, and adversity. They are proven, rock-solid, and trustworthy. Building on these concepts will take you down the path of creating enduring organizations and legacies.

- What do you fear most about becoming an enduring leader? What is it you cannot let go of?
- What do you fear about building enduring teams? What is it you cannot let go of?
- Without an enduring foundation of trust, it will be difficult to build a trusting leadership style. What is the foundation of your trust?

A Legacy of Trust

W e *trust* you are now convinced that there is a time-tested, better way to become a leader who others want to follow.

Since all of us have been concentrating so hard on this book's content, isn't it time for a little break? Let's talk about golf!

Golf is an enigma. (Now there's a classic understatement!) Former PGA tour member Gardner Dickinson once said, "They say golf is like life, but don't believe them. It's more complicated than that."

The sport abounds with perplexity and paradox: fairway and rough, dry land and water, green and sand trap. And then there are all the complexities involving mind and body.

Most of us are born with an arm/hand preference. Some of us are right-handed; others are left-handed. Golf says, "Don't use what comes naturally! Let your other hand (your out-of-preference side) pull the swing through the ball." For example, for many players their right hand is dominant in all other aspects of their lives. But in golf, if they allow the right hand to control their golf swing, the ball hooks—hello rough. However, if they learn to use their left hand effectively—a new swing style—they will hit the ball straighter and have lower scores (which, of course, in golf is *better*).

Isn't that just like leadership? If we allow our dominant preferences to always be in control, we will often not have complete success. However, we can learn to adjust our style away from a dominant (and in some cases damaging) preference and become better leaders if we are willing to make some changes.

To be successful in golf, players need to learn how to overcome or "position" their natural tendencies (or preferences) in order to hit just the right shot.

This is also true with leadership. We look for and focus on our strengths, but we are better leaders when we also allow other qualities to develop and come to the forefront. For example, it is not natural for many of us to be humble team builders. It is much easier to strive for the attention of others and build a personal résumé, ignoring the team's input and value. But by intentional effort we can learn to be humble and at the same time increase our success as a leader.

The temptation will always be to head in the other direction—toward the dominant preferences inside us and on every side in our environment.

Over the last several years, investors suddenly began looking for CEOs who could shake things up and put an end to what was perceived as a business-as-usual approach. A new breed of corporate leader emerged: the charismatic CEO. A fervent and often irrational faith in the power of dynamic leaders became part of our culture.

Rakesh Khurana writes,

> Faith is an invaluable, even indispensable gift in human affairs.... In the
> sphere of business, the faith of entrepreneurs, leaders, and ordinary
> employees in a company, a product, or an idea can unleash tremendous
> amounts of innovation and productivity. Yet today's extraordinary trust
> in the power of the charismatic CEO resembles less a mature faith than
> it does a belief in magic. If, however, we are willing to begin rethinking
> our ideas about leadership, the age of faith can be followed by an era of
> faith and reason.[1]

The adventure of looking for the charismatic leader sometimes asked us to turn our backs on attributes such as honesty, integrity, sensitivity, commitment, achievement, nurturing, trustworthiness, peacemaking, and courage.

But as Jim Collins explained so convincingly in his best-selling book *Good to Great,* it is the noncharismatic leader who seems to endure and shine in the long run. Collins writes:

> Compared to high-profile leaders with big personalities who make headlines and become celebrities, the good-to-great leaders [leaders who have taken companies to unprecedented long-term growth] seem to have come from Mars. Self-effacing, quiet, reserved, even shy—these leaders are a paradoxical blend of personal humility and professional will. They are more like Lincoln and Socrates than Patton or Caesar.[2]

In this book we have outlined eight attributes of a truly great leader. We have referred to two of those attributes as the pillars: *humility* and *endurance.* Focusing on these two pillars is like so many things (golf included) that are both simple and complex. However, our experience tells us that great leaders allow these two attributes, whether natural or not, to strongly influence their leadership style. They learn how to overcome or "position" their natural tendencies. They let the two pillars "pull them through" their swing of everyday leadership and team building.

Great leaders seek to be humble people who lift up others and keep the spotlight on their companies, not themselves. They have a burning ambition to see tasks completed, and they balance that desire with a deep concern for the growth and development of people. They want to nurture relationships, help others flourish, and shove the fuss away from themselves.

Pressure and mounting fear can drive you away from the two pillars in order to succeed in the short run, but it will not last or create trust. It will only drive a wedge between you and the true success you can have as a leader who focuses on the two pillars and the other attributes.

Once again we want to remind you of the power contained in these qualities—and how the opposite qualities can destroy the great person you want to become and the great organization you want to lead.

We all have the ability to adapt these attributes to our particular leadership styles. You have the ability to start today. Why wait any longer?

Grasping leadership greatness starts by letting go:

If we do not let go, we make prisoners of ourselves....
Let go of the strategies that have worked for us in the past...
Let go of our biases, the foundation of our illusions...
Let go of our grievances, the root source of victimhood...
Let go of our so-often-denied fear...[3]

Letting go is not a one-time deal. You must do it again and again and again.

Many of the most enduring ideas and values in our lives today have been shaped and molded by modern-day "blacksmiths." Ancient or modern, the principles are the same: The blacksmith heats the iron at the forge, shapes it on his anvil, and cools it in the water.

The blacksmith heats the metal to prepare it for change. The trusted leader warms people to change through humility and compassion. The blacksmith hammers the metal to form a new shape. The trusted leader shapes an organization through commitment and focus. The blacksmith cools the metal to "settle" its strength. The trusted leader uses peacemaking to give the changed organization meaning and understanding. The forged metal, once cooled, becomes the powerful sword, the productive plow, or the beautiful wrought-iron gate.

By understanding the elements that build and destroy trust, effective leaders shape strong and productive organizations:

TRUST-DESTROYING ELEMENTS	TRUST-BUILDING ELEMENTS
PRIDE is a focus on yourself. It brings an air of arrogance. Prideful people resist change and create a selfish work environment.	**HUMILITY** is a focus on being open, teachable, and flexible.
JUDGMENTAL leaders are intolerant and critical and create a negative work or team environment.	**DEVELOPMENT** guides leaders to nurture and mentor people and then let them go.
WILLFULNESS leads to a lack of commitment, dedication, and respect. Willful leaders exhibit stubbornness based on pride.	**COMMITMENT** seeks to develop vision and values; it moves leaders to stand for something greater.
STAGNATION carries with it purposelessness, apathy, and scattered attention. It can lead to laziness, uncontrolled thoughts, and lack of vision.	**FOCUS** gives leaders the ability to achieve, have passion, and direct their time and energies to the important things.
INSENSITIVITY is a lack of concern for others. Insensitive leaders do not listen and are unconcerned and indifferent about others.	**COMPASSION** is a desire to serve, understand others, and care for people, the organization, and the community.
DISHONESTY exposes devious leaders. They deny reality and have an incongruence in their lives that causes masked behavior.	**INTEGRITY** demands that leaders be authentic and seek to create quality not only in the products or services they produce but in relationships as well.
DIVISIVENESS brings fear and anxiety to an organization. Conflicts are not resolved, and destructive behaviors lead teams to fight among themselves.	**PEACEMAKING** leaders bring calm to their organizations by learning from and honoring others and seeking good solutions rather than quickly made, bad decisions.
AVOIDANCE OF SUFFERING guides organizations to always look for the easy way out. Teams and organizations avoid problems, responsibility, and difficulties.	**ENDURANCE** speaks to courage, perseverance, and holding strong when events, people, or the environment become difficult.

At the end of the same session when Jesus shared his Beatitudes with his followers—the ideas on which the eight attributes are based—he told an interesting story. Jesus said that if his team members would put what he had taught them into practice, their lives would be like a man who built his house on a solid rock foundation. No matter what kind of storm hit, Jesus promised that the house would stand. But if these men did not pay attention to the truth Jesus shared, their lives would be like the man who built his house on a foundation of shifting sand. When the storm hit that house, it would crumble and wash away.[4]

We believe the eight attributes will have that kind of effect on you. Allow them to permeate you from the inside out, and you will have a career—and a life—built on solid rock. You will be known as a person who can say with clear-eyed conviction, "Trust me."

And others will follow.

Notes

Chapter 1: The Way of Trust

1. Warren Bennis, "The Leadership Advantage," *Leader to Leader,* no. 12 (spring 1999).
2. Robert E. Quinn, *Deep Change* (Hoboken, N.J.: John Wiley & Sons, 1996), xiv.

Humility

1. Jim Collins, *Good to Great: Why Some Companies Make the Leap and Others Don't* (New York: HarperCollins, 2001), 21.

Chapter 2: Feet on the Ground

1. Peter Senge, quoted in Alan M. Webber, "Learning for a Change," *Fast Company,* no. 24 (May 1999): 178.
2. Proverbs 11:2, NLT.
3. Monci J. Williams, "Agility in Learning: An Essential for Evolving Organizations—and People," *Harvard Management Update* 2, no. 5 (May 1997). Copyright 1997 by the Harvard Business School Publishing Corporation. Reprinted by permission of *Harvard Management Update.* All rights reserved.
4. Howard Hendricks, *Teaching to Change Lives: Seven Proven Ways to Make Your Teaching Come Alive* (Sisters, Oreg.: Multnomah, 1987), 32.

5. Robert E. Quinn, *Deep Change* (Hoboken, N.J.: John Wiley & Sons, 1996).

CHAPTER 3: FINDING SPARKY

1. David Michaelis, *Passages: The Life and Times of Charles Schulz.* Found at www.schulzmuseum.org/schulzbio.html.
2. From Greg Haines, Internet Obituary Network. Found at www.obits.com.
3. James 1:19, NLT.
4. From Wayne Rice, *Hot Illustrations for Youth Talks* (Grand Rapids: Zondervan, 1994).

DEVELOPMENT

1. C. William Pollard, *The Soul of the Firm* (Grand Rapids: Zondervan, 1996), 113.
2. Matthew 7:3.

CHAPTER 4: LETTING GO

1. Matthew 7:1-2, NLT.
2. From Daniel Goleman, *Emotional Intelligence* (New York: Bantam Books, 1995), 81-82.
3. James M. Kouzes and Barry Z. Posner, *The Leadership Challenge: How to Keep Getting Extraordinary Things Done in Organizations* (Hoboken, N.J.: John Wiley & Sons, 1995), 69.
4. Tom Peters, *Thriving on Chaos: Handbook for a Management Revolution* (New York: Knopf, 1987), 261.

CHAPTER 5: THICK-AND-THIN TOGETHERNESS

1. Michael Dell, as quoted in James M. Citrin, "Six Principles for Leading During Uncertain Times," *Business 2.0,* 31 January 2002.
2. David W. Smith, *The Friendless American Male* (Ventura, Calif.: Gospel Light, 1983), 85.
3. Bernice R. Sandler, "Women as Mentors: Myths and Commandments," *The Chronicle of Higher Education,* 10 March 1993. Found at www.bernicesandler.com.
4. Interview with director Frank Darabont, "Walking the Mile," prod. and dir. Constantine Z. Nasr, Zelt Productions, 1999, behind-the-scenes documentary.
5. Jim Collins, *Good to Great: Why Some Companies Make the Leap and Others Don't* (New York: HarperCollins, 2001), 51.
6. Charles R. Swindoll, *Dropping Your Guard* (Waco, Tex.: Word, 1983), 171.
7. Proverbs 27:6, NLT.

COMMITMENT

1.*Braveheart,* dir. Mel Gibson, Twentieth Century Fox, 1995.

CHAPTER 6: CLIMBING ABOVE THE FOG

1. Matthew 6:21.
2. Stephen R. Covey, *The 7 Habits of Highly Effective People* (New York: Simon & Schuster, The Free Press, 1989), 32.
3. Warren G. Bennis and Burt Nanus, *Leaders: The Strategies for Taking Charge* (New York, HarperCollins, 1985), 89.

4. Bennis and Nanus, *Leaders,* 111.

5. James M. Kouzes and Barry Z. Posner, *The Leadership Challenge: How to Keep Getting Extraordinary Things Done in Organizations* (Hoboken, N.J.: John Wiley & Sons, 1995), 96.

6. John P. Kotter, *Leading Change* (Boston: Harvard Business School Press, 1996), 51-52.

7. From J. Chapman, "Collegial Support Linked to Reduction of Job Stress," *Nursing Management* 24, no. 5 (1993): 52-54.

Chapter 7: Standing for Something Greater

1. M. Scott Peck, *The Road Less Traveled* (New York: Simon & Schuster, 1985).

2. Doug Linder, "The Trial of Susan B. Anthony for Illegal Voting," 2001. Found at www.law.umkc.edu/faculty/projects/ftrials/anthony.

3. Linder, "The Trial of Susan B. Anthony."

4. Based on multiple sources, including www.rochester.edu/SBA/ friendship, www.susanbanthonyhouse.org, and William H. Harris and Judith S. Levey, eds., "Susan Brownell Anthony," *The New Columbia Encyclopedia* (New York: Columbia University Press, 1975), 116.

5. From Barry Z. Posner and R. I. Westwood, "An International Perspective on Shared Values" (paper presented at the Western Academy of Management International Conference, Brisbane, Australia, July 1994).

6. From John P. Kotter and James L. Heskett, *Corporate Culture and Performance* (New York: Simon & Schuster, The Free Press, 1992).

7. Joyce Meyer, *A Leader in the Making* (Tulsa, Okla.: Harrison House, 2001), 82.

8. James M. Kouzes and Barry Z. Posner, *The Leadership Challenge: How to Keep Getting Extraordinary Things Done in Organizations* (Hoboken, N.J.: John Wiley & Sons, 1995), 338. Four moral goals of Leadership taken from John W. Gardner, *Leadership Papers 5: The Moral Aspect of Leadership* (Washington, D.C.: Independent Sector, 1987), 10-18.

9. John McCain, "Duty, Honor, Country." Speech given at the Republican National Convention August 15, 1988. Found at www.ipledgeallegiancetothe.us.mccain.html.

10. McCain, "Duty, Honor, Country."

Focus

1. Matthew 6:24.

Chapter 8: Doing the Right Things Right

1. Keith H. Hammonds, "You Can Do Anything—But Not Everything," *Fast Company*, no. 34 (May 2000): 206.

2. David Allen, quoted in Hammonds, *Fast Company*, 206.

3. Daniel Phillips submitted this statement in response to an entry question asked during the 2001 Global Readers' Challenge by *Fast Company* magazine, a contest to identify the "Fast 50 Trendsetters."

4. Robert K. Cooper, *The Other 90%: How to Unlock Your Vast Untapped Potential for Leadership and Life* (New York: Crown, 2001), 135-36.

5. Information for this story was gathered from Robert K. Cooper, *The Other 90%*, 135-36.

6. David C. McClelland, "Three Basic Approaches to Improving Productivity: Achievement Motivation." Found at www.accel-team. com/human_relations/hrels_06_mcclelland.html. Used by permission.

Chapter 9: Keeping the Band in Tune

1. Ron Rex submitted this statement in response to an entry question asked during the 2001Global Readers' Challenge by *Fast Company* magazine, a contest to identify the "Fast 50 Trendsetters."
2. The Time Management Matrix, excerpted from Stephen R. Covey, *The 7 Habits of Highly Effective People* (New York: Simon & Schuster, The Free Press, 1989), 151. Copyright © 1989 Franklin Covey Co. Reprinted with permission. All rights reserved.
3. Al Ries, "Focus, Focus, Focus," *Inc.,* November 1996. Found at www.inc.com/magazine/19961101/1877.html.
4. Ram Charan, "Why CEOs Fail," *Fortune,* 21 June 1999.
5. Larry Bossidy and Ram Charan, *Execution: The Discipline of Getting Things Done* (New York: Crown, 2002), 6.
6. From Thomas Gilbert, *Human Competence: Engineering Worthy Performance* (Silver Spring, Md.: McGraw-Hill, International Society for Performance Improvement, 1996), 56.
7. James M. Kouzes and Barry Z. Posner, *The Leadership Challenge: How to Keep Getting Extraordinary Things Done in Organizations* (Hoboken, N.J.: John Wiley & Sons, 1995), 124.
8. Core Qualities chart, excerpted from Daniel Ofman, *Core Qualties: A Gateway to Human Resources* (Holland: Scriptum, 2001). Used by permission. All rights reserved. For more information, go to www.corequadrants.com and www.corequalities.com.

COMPASSION

1. James S. Hewett, *Illustrations Unlimited* (Wheaton, Ill.: Tyndale, 1988), 119.
2. Matthew 25:40.
3. J. Oswald Sanders, *Spiritual Leadership* (Chicago: Moody, 1967), 185.

CHAPTER 10: "I CARE"

1. Donald T. Phillips, *Lincoln on Leadership: Executive Strategies for Tough Times* (New York: Warner Books, 1992), 34.
2. Luke 10:34. For further details on the story of the good Samaritan, read Luke 10:30-35.
3. Tom Peters and Nancy Austin, *A Passion for Excellence* (New York: Random House, 1985), 30.
4. Pat Williams, *Mr. Littlejohn's Secrets to a Lifetime of Success* (Grand Rapids: Revell, 2000), 47.
5. Jim L. Wilson, *Fresh Illustrations*. Found at www.freshministry.org. Used by permission.
6. Proverbs 25:11-12, NLT.

CHAPTER 11: "YOU FIRST"

1. Bert Frizen story by Chuck Holsinger as told by Lynn McAdam, *Leadership Journal* 18, no. 4 (fall 1997). Used by permission.
2. James M. Kouzes and Barry Z. Posner, *The Leadership Challenge: How to Keep Getting Extraordinary Things Done in Organizations* (Hoboken, N.J.: John Wiley & Sons, 1995), 184.

3. Robert K. Greenleaf, "The Servant as Leader" (Indianapolis: The Greenleaf Center, 1970; reprint 1991), 20. For more information, go to www.greenleaf.org.
4. Adapted from material by Ann McGee-Cooper, Ed.D., "Accountability as Covenant: The Taproot of Servant Leadership." Used by permission of AMCA, Inc., Dallas, Texas.

INTEGRITY

1. From James M. Kouzes and Barry Z. Posner, *Credibility: How Leaders Gain and Lose It, Why People Demand It* (Hoboken, N.J.: John Wiley & Sons, 1995), 14.
2. Bruce Horovitz, "Trust in Corporations Waning in Wake of Scandals," *USA Today,* 16 July 2002.
3. From John A. Byrne, "Commentary: No Excuses for Enron's Board," *BusinessWeek Online,* 29 July 2002.
4. Matthew 6:21.

CHAPTER 12: THE REAL DEAL

1. C. William Pollard, *The Soul of the Firm* (Grand Rapids: Zondervan, 1996), 66.
2. October 15, 1951, address given by Harry S. Truman at the groundbreaking ceremonies at Wake Forest College, Winston-Salem, North Carolina. See *Public Papers of the Presidents of the United States, Harry S. Truman, 1951: Containing the Public Messages, Speeches, and Statements of the President, January 1 to December 31, 1951* (Washington, D. C.: GPO, 1999). Also found at www.trumanlibrary.org.
3. *Spider-Man,* dir. Sam Raimi, Columbia Pictures, 2002.

4. Stephen R. Covey, *The 7 Habits of Highly Effective People* (New York: Simon & Schuster, The Free Press, 1989), 98.

5. See Peter Drucker, *The Drucker Foundation: The Leader of the Future* (Hoboken, N.J.: John Wiley & Sons, 1996).

6. Robert J. Rotella, *Golf Is Not a Game of Perfect* (New York: Simon & Schuster, 1995), 126.

7. Stephen R. Covey, "Taproot of Trust," Franklin Covey Corporation, December 1991. Also found at www.franklin covey.com.

8. Robert K. Cooper, *The Other 90%: How to Unlock Your Vast Untapped Potential for Leadership and Life* (New York: Crown, 2001), 47.

CHAPTER 13: TRUSTING ONE ANOTHER

1. J. W. Driscoll, "Trust and Participation in Organizational Decision Making as Predictors of Satisfaction," *Academy of Management Journal* 21, no. 1 (1978): 44-56.

2. Charles A. O'Reilly and Karlene H. Roberts, "Information Filtration in Organizations: Three Experiments," *Organizational Behavior and Human Performance* 11 (1974): 253-65.

3. From W. R. Boss, "Trust and Managerial Problem Solving Revisited," *Group and Organizational Studies* 3, no. 3 (1978): 331-42.

4. Donald T. Phillips, *Lincoln on Leadership: Executive Strategies for Tough Times* (New York: Warner Books, 1992), 18.

5. Mike Hoffman, "The Leader Within," *Inc.,* September 1998. Used by permission.

6. John C. Maxwell, *The Maxwell Leadership Bible: Developing Leaders from the Word of God* (Nashville: Nelson, 2002), 1437.

7. Tom Peters, "Learning to Love Change" (TPG Communications), 1990. Found at www.tompeters.com.

8. "Building Trust," *Inc.,* 1 August 1990. Used by permission.

9. Tom Peters and Nancy Austin, *A Passion for Excellence* (New York: Random House, 1985), 98.

10. Thomas Stewart, "A Conversation with Joseph Juran," *Fortune,* 1 January 1999. Found at www.business2.com.

Peacemaking

1. James M. Citrin, "Maybe It's Time to Slow Down," *Business 2.0,* 31 July 2002.

2. John 14:27.

Chapter 14: Calming Chaos

1. Stuart Kauffman, *At Home in the Universe: The Search for the Laws of Self-Organization and Complexity* (New York: Oxford University Press, 1996).

2. Margaret J. Wheatley, *Leadership and the New Science: Learning About Organization from an Orderly Universe* (San Francisco: Berrett-Koehler, 1992).

3. James M. Kouzes and Barry Z. Posner, *The Leadership Challenge: How to Keep Getting Extraordinary Things Done in Organizations* (Hoboken, N.J.: John Wiley & Sons, 1995), 76.

4. From Marilyn Elias, "Proud to Be an American Even with the Jitters," USA Today *Online,* 11 October 2001.

5. Elisabeth Kübler-Ross, *On Death and Dying* (New York: MacMillan, 1969), 263.

6. Lucy McCauley and Christine Canabou, "The Voice of Experience," *Fast Company,* no. 46 (May 2001), 79.

7. Max Lucado, *The Applause of Heaven* (Nashville: W Publishing, 1996), 127.

Chapter 15: Dream Team

1. Peter F. Drucker, *Management Challenges for the 21st Century* (New York: HarperCollins, 2001).
2. Chuck Daly quoted in John Gettings, "Olympics Dream Team: Every NBA Fan's Dream Turns to Gold." Found at www.fact monster/spot/mm-nba.html. Used by permission.
3. Tom Peters, " 'Team at the Top' Proves to Be a Misnomer," 20 May 1988. Found at www.tompeters.com/toms_world/ t1988/052088-team.asp.
4. From Michael Gershman, *Getting It Right the Second Time* (Boston: Addison-Wesley Longman, 1991).
5. John P. Kotter, *Leading Change* (Boston: Harvard Business School Press, 1996), 99.
6. J. R. R. Tolkien, *The Fellowship of the Ring* (Boston: Houghton Mifflin, 2003).
7. Kenneth W. Thomas and Ralph H. Kilmann, "Thomas-Kilmann Conflict Mode Instrument: Profile and Interpretive Report" (Xicom, Inc., Consulting Psychologists Press), 1974, 2001.
8. Adapted from Thomas and Kilmann, "Thomas-Kilmann Conflict Mode Instrument," 1974, 2001.
9. Alan L. McGinnis, *Bringing Out the Best in People* (Minneapolis: Augsburg, 1985).
10. Peter Senge, *The Fifth Discipline* (New York: Doubleday, 1990).
11. Tom Peters, "No Short Cuts," 29 May 1987. Found at www. tompeters.com/toms_world/t1987/052987-no.asp.

12. From Brian Palmer, Jeff Flock, and Jeff Goodell, "Quecreek Miner Miracle: Teamwork Helped Miners Survive Underground," 28 July 2002. Found at www.CNN.com/2002/US/07/28/mine-accident.

13. James M. Kouzes and Barry Z. Posner, *The Leadership Challenge: How to Keep Getting Extraordinary Things Done in Organizations* (Hoboken, N.J.: John Wiley & Sons, 1995), 170.

ENDURANCE

1. The sources for this story were the original manuscript account and a report found at http://myhero.com/hero.asp?hero=stevefossett.

CHAPTER 16: STANDING STRONG

1. Greg Sandoval, "CDNow Shareholders Revolt with Lawsuit," 25 August 2000. Found at news.com.com/2100-1017_3-244968.html?tag=mainstry.

2. M. Scott Peck, *The Road Less Traveled* (New York: Simon & Schuster, 1985), 17.

3. Found at quotesheaven.com/by_author/churchill_sirwinston/page4.html.

4. From "Bunker Mentality: What's Inside a Real Panic Room?" 2 April 2002. Found at abcnews.go.com/GMA/GoodMorningAmerica/GMA020402Panic_rooms_real.html.

5. From "Col. Harland Sanders: American Fast Food Pioneer." Found at www.ajskfc.com/colsanders.html.

6. "Col. Harland Sanders: American Fast Food Pioneer." Found at www.ajskfc.com/colsanders.html.

7. Stan Toler, *God Has Never Failed Me: But He's Sure Scared Me to Death a Few Times* (Tulsa, Okla.: Honor Books, 1999).

8. The Voice of the Martyrs, *Heroic Faith: How to Live a Life of Extreme Devotion* (Nashville: W Publishing, 2002), 78. Reprinted by permission. All rights reserved.

CHAPTER 17: THE ENDURING ORGANIZATION

1. The Daughters of the Republic of Texas, "The Alamo's Historic Past." Found at http://www.thealamo.org/history/historicpast.html.

2. From "Alamo," *The New Columbia Encyclopedia* (New York: Columbia University Press, 1975), 46.

3. The Daughters of the Republic of Texas, "The Alamo's Historic Past." Found at http://www.thealamo.org/history/historicpast.html.

4. From www.lsjunction.com/events/alamo.

5. Noel M. Tichy and Eli B. Cohen, *The Leadership Engine: How Winning Companies Build Leaders at Every Level* (New York: Harper-Collins, 1997), 238.

6. James 1:2-4, NLT.

7. Julien R. Phillips and Allan A. Kennedy, "Shaping and Managing Shared Values," McKinsey Staff Paper (December 1980): 8.

8. Chattanooga Resource Foundation, "Perseverance Illustrations." Found at www.resourcefoundation.org/Community/Schools/Persev-i.shtml. Used by permission.

9. Found at www.theotherpages.org/quote.html.

CHAPTER 18: A LEGACY OF TRUST

1. Rakesh Khurana, "The Curse of the Superstar CEO," *Harvard Business Review*, 1 September 2002.

2. Jim Collins, *Good to Great: Why Some Companies Make the Leap, and Others Don't* (New York: HarperCollins, 2001), 12.

3. Gordon MacKenzie, *Orbiting the Giant Hairball: A Corporate Fool's Guide to Surviving with Grace* (New York: Viking Penguin, 1998), 216.

4. See Matthew 7:24-29.

About the Authors

WAYNE HASTINGS, a sought-after author, speaker, and business consultant, delivers one of the most critical messages in business today: trust. Through exhaustive research and years of hands-on experience, Wayne illuminates timeless principles necessary for inspiring leadership, team building, and organizational development. As a speaker and trainer, Wayne shares powerful alternatives to today's floundering business tactics by offering simple yet paradigm-shifting concepts for leaders across a wide range of industries. A respected business leader for more than thirty years, Wayne has firsthand experience in areas such as publishing, retail, wholesale, distribution, and inventory management.

Wayne is the president of The Wayne Hastings Company, an organization committed to transforming organizations by changing people through a teaching style rooted in heart and truth. Wayne and his wife, Pam, have two married children and reside in Arroyo Grande, California.

To learn more about how Wayne can serve your organization's needs, visit www.waynehastings.com, or e-mail him at info@waynehastings.com.

RON POTTER'S expertise in organizational effectiveness is an outgrowth of more than thirty years in corporate leadership positions. An entrepreneur and consultant, he offers skills that represent a rich mix of practical experience spanning the fields of executive management, marketing and sales, project management and computer technology. Ron has worked with a wide range of clients as a facilitator, consultant, coach, and mentor. His work includes leadership development, team building, and corporate culture growth with executives and leaders in industries such as auto manufacturing, computers, distribution, engineering and technology, food manufacturing, and pharmaceuticals.

Since graduating from the University of Michigan, Ron has forged a successful and diverse career, moving from university classrooms to corporate boardrooms. His company, Team Leadership Culture, guides businesses in new directions and to new heights by focusing and improving the performance of organizational leaders, their team dynamics, and the corporate culture they create and perpetuate.

To learn more about how Ron's consulting company can transform your business, visit www.tlcllc.com, or e-mail him at rpotter@tlcllc.com.